KV-026-258

WITHDRAWN   WITHDRAWN

**This book is to be returned on or before
the last date stamped below.**

CANCELLED

CANCELLED

CANCELLED

CANCELLED

CANCELLED

31 NOV 1983

CANCELLED

CANCELLED

13 DEC 1985

-7 FEB 1986

28 NOV 1986

19 FEB 1986

24. APR 1995

FARNHAM, W.

The Shakespearean grotesque

92,196

057781

THE
SHAKESPEAREAN
GROTESQUE

LIBRARY

ACC. No. DEPT.

CLASS No.

822.33 A2 FAR

UNIVERSITY
COLLEGE CHESTER

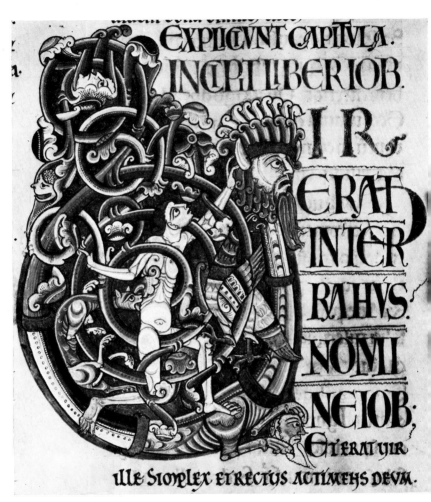

Mankind within the Grotesque

An initial 'V' for the Book of Job in a Vulgate Bible, MS. Auct. E. inf. 1, fol. 304ʳ; English, late twelfth century

THE
SHAKESPEAREAN
GROTESQUE

Its Genesis and Transformations

BY

WILLARD FARNHAM

PADGATE
COLLEGE OF EDUCATION
LIBRARY
ACC. NO. 92,196.

OXFORD
AT THE CLARENDON PRESS
1971

Oxford University Press, Ely House, London W. 1

GLASGOW NEW YORK TORONTO MELBOURNE WELLINGTON
CAPE TOWN SALISBURY IBADAN NAIROBI DAR ES SALAAM LUSAKA ADDIS ABABA
BOMBAY CALCUTTA MADRAS KARACHI LAHORE DACCA
KUALA LUMPUR SINGAPORE HONG KONG TOKYO

© OXFORD UNIVERSITY PRESS 1971

PRINTED IN GREAT BRITAIN

13413

To F. F.
who knows

PREFACE

To write about the grotesque as I have written here is to become growingly conscious of ways in which it can help to join age to age within a culture and yet take on distinctive quality in any one age. The reader familiar with the grotesque in Shakespeare and also in literature and other art of the present time will have his own ideas about relationship between grotesque forms from two very different ages of our post-classical western world. That such a reader will find some relationship, much or little, is to be expected. It is for him to decide how near Shakespeare comes to what is now known as the theatre of the absurd, for example, or how far away he stands from it even as he provides in part for its being.

Portions of this book have been incorporated in two public lectures given in 1964, one at the University of Wisconsin at Madison and the other at Rice University. The second lecture was part of a programme commemorating the four-hundredth anniversary of the births of Shakespeare and Marlowe. I wish to thank the Department of English at each of those universities for most memorable kindnesses shown me as a visitor.

I also wish to thank two libraries, the Bodleian at Oxford and the British Museum, for their gracious extension of aid and privileges to me while this book was being written. To both libraries I have been long indebted for many earlier courtesies.

WILLARD FARNHAM

Berkeley, California
September 29, 1969

CONTENTS

LIST OF ILLUSTRATIONS

I

BEAUTIFUL DEFORMITY

1

THERE is a well-known comment made by St. Bernard of Clairvaux upon a manifestation of the grotesque in religious art of his day. Both for that which it contains and for that which it significantly does not contain this comment may be considered at the beginning of what is here to be said about the formation of the Shakespearean grotesque. The world of the grotesque familiar to St. Bernard, with its prevalent monstrous forms, is a distant but valid precursor of the early Shakespearean world of the grotesque that is dominated by the monstrous form of Falstaff.

The time is about 1125, and St. Bernard, the austere founder of the Cistercian monastic order, may seem to be a saintly Philistine as he finds much to say against artistic splendour in churches and disapproves especially of grotesque cloister decorations, such as those provided lavishly by the Cluniac order. Churches, he says, are resplendent in their walls at the cost of being beggarly in their poor. The art they display to the public may, of course, show love for the dwelling-place of God's honour, and it is not harmful to those lay folk who are simple and devout. But it is harmful to those who are vain and covetous. As for the monks, who are spiritual folk, why put before their eyes, as they read and meditate in the cloister, a mass of fantastic art? For them 'what profit is there in that ridiculous monstrosity, a marvellous kind of deformed beauty and beautiful deformity?' (*quid facit illa ridicula monstruositas, mira quaedam deformis formositas, ac formosa deformitas?*)[1]

---

[1] Quotations from the Latin text are from *Patrologia Latina*, ed. J.-P. Migne, Paris, 1844–55, clxxxii, col. 916. The entire passage of comment, which is from St. Bernard's *Apologia ad Guillelmum Sancti-Theoderici Abbatem*, is translated in *A Medieval Garner*, ed. G. G. Coulton, London, 1910, pp. 71–2.

Quickly enough it begins to appear that St. Bernard is not
exactly insensitive to religious art. Rather he finds things to say
against it because he knows something of the appeal it can have
and thinks it gets in the way of matters that for him are more important. Most notable is an appeal which he claims the grotesque
in religious art has for cloistered monks. This amounts to an enticement away from religious meditation and toward aesthetic
meditation. Why should the grotesques in the cloister be presented by the sculptor as beauty in a religious setting? And can
they *mean* anything in that setting? By such questions, he implies,
a susceptible monk can be challenged. The beauty presented is
strange enough to be called deformity and the deformity strange
enough to be called beauty. However much St. Bernard himself
may be proof against the enticement to this kind of meditation, he
appears to recognize it as more than a temptation to engage in
idle wonder. He appears to make it a temptation for a questing
spirit. He says: 'In short, so many and so marvellous are the varie-
ties of divers shapes on every hand that we are more tempted to
read in the marble than in our books and to spend the whole day
in wondering at these things rather than in meditating the law of
God. For God's sake, if men are not ashamed of these follies, why
at least do they not shrink from the expense?' (*si non pudet inepti-
arum, cur vel non piget expensarum?*)

About the divers shapes to be found in the marble St. Bernard
is specific. Among them are monsters such as centaurs, other half-
men, a four-footed beast with a serpent's tail, a fish with a beast's
head, a body with many heads, a head with many bodies, and
a beast half horse and half goat. Among them are also non-
monstrous beasts such as apes, lions, and tigers. In addition there
are non-monstrous men who hunt or fight in this world where
monsters are so easily formed out of beasts and men.

We might expect the figures to be what they are described as
being, since we are familiar with their kind in much medieval
church decoration and much medieval manuscript illumination.
There is about their use in grotesque art a spirit that asks to be
called anything from fantastically ominous to fancifully gay,

according to what its temper seems to be in the range between
non-humorous and humorous. It is notable that in what St.
Bernard says about such cloister decoration he cannot be suspected
of condemning it as being humorous and therefore out of place
in its setting, except possibly when he sees in it a *ridicula monstruositas*. But what he thus calls ridiculous he appears elsewhere
to be thinking of as outlandish rather than comic. The wonderment that he fears meditating monks will be led into by it is not
indicated as wonderment at the giving of the comic a place in
religious art. It is to be remembered, of course, that in the grotesque of St. Bernard's time we ourselves often find it hard to discover humour that we can be sure of, though such discovery
becomes more and more possible in the medieval grotesque of
later centuries.

If St. Bernard thinks of certain earnest monks as being led to
search for religious symbolism as they 'read in' the marble of
cloister grotesques, he probably judges their search to be vain.
Émile Mâle would largely discourage present-day searching of
that kind when, in *L'Art religieux du XIIIᵉ siècle en France*, he refers
to this passage of St. Bernard's.[1] Mâle uses the passage to support
his contention that though the age of St. Bernard was well able
to make the unicorn stand symbolically for Christ, the phoenix
for the Resurrection, the basilisk for death, the dragon for the
devil, and other such figures to serve symbolic purpose likewise,
it usually created in an utterly different spirit the kind of grotesque
decoration St. Bernard describes. The age was content, he thinks,
that such decoration should be the result of giving free rein to an
imagination that was encouraged by casual knowledge of representations of animals and monsters in arts of the past. There is
much for Mâle to base his judgement on. It seems indeed that
animals and monsters of the Romanesque decorative grotesque
do not as a rule come into being because of symbolic conceptions

---

[1] 3rd edn., 'revue et augmentée', Paris, 1910, pp. 65–8. Equally strong dis-
couragement of such searching in Romanesque church decoration where combats
of men and 'uncouth animals' are presented is to be found in a more recent comment by Lawrence Stone, *Sculpture in Britain: The Middle Ages*, Harmondsworth,
1955, p. 54.

like those of the bestiaries. Moreover, in the figurations of animals, monsters, and men in the medieval grotesque as a whole we find a sensibility that is less and less like that of bestiary symbolism, however persistently the bestiary creatures remain in men's memories and suggest uses to the artist. It is a sensibility with less and less of the other-worldliness that finds the true significance of things elsewhere than in the here and now.

However much the decorative grotesque of the early Middle Ages may properly be called extraneous, there is in it a moving spirit that is destined to be passed on to a later, more developed, grotesque art and to work against extraneousness in that art. This spirit comes to work thus because it is preoccupied with dramatically opposed forces in life, which more and more have recognition as the Renaissance turns toward and explores the natural world. It makes the grotesque sensible of, and impels it to represent, pervasive conflict in nature. The conflict as represented has its simpler aspects in brutal combat between living beings. It shows subtler aspects when a man or an animal strives against a twisted entanglement implying intricacy in nature or when a monster seems to be the result of a breaking down of normal creatures and a recombination of parts of them in a form where the parts must be at war with each other in their incongruity.

Before the formation of the Shakespearean grotesque a further conflict comes to be plain. This is between the grotesque itself and that to which it is attached as decoration or with which it joins when it becomes more than decoration. In the Romanesque period some struggle must be taken to exist between grotesque decoration and the non-grotesque religious art which it decorates, even though St. Bernard directs attention to such decoration because it brings into existence not this struggle within art but one between art and religion in the thoughts of a monk, who should rather be freeing himself from susceptibility to art. But in the Gothic period there is an aesthetic struggle which asks very plainly to be recognized when a spirit of comedy grows within the grotesque. Medieval English drama shows one manifestation of that struggle as development begins of a closer and closer joining, and at the same time a more and more significant opposition between low comedy and high seriousness. The supreme result of this development comes in what Shakespeare does with low comedy in conjunction with high comedy as well as with high seriousness.

2

The Renaissance grotesque, in which the Shakespearean grotesque has its setting, is like much else in the Renaissance in that it grows from a medieval creative spirit. As it grows it is worked on by stimulating and modifying influences that come from discovery of classic forms of the imagination in the ancient world. It is the more impelled to make the discovery by the fact that the medieval grotesque, even from its Romanesque beginning, like medieval art generally, builds in part upon late classic forms passed on to it. Among these forms there are, for example, monsters like centaurs, sirens, mermaids, and so-called grylles (heads with no bodies but with limbs directly joined).[1] There are also certain forms of containing design. But the way in which such forms are used becomes more and more distinct from the classic. That the medieval creative spirit itself did not spring into being without a background is of course to be recognized. How far back one should go for what can properly be taken as intimations of its formation has come to be more and more a question. But demonstration is offered in support of the argument that upon occasion 'sub-antique' art of the late classical world 'anticipates that complete negation of the principles of classical art which the early Middle Ages were gradually to exemplify'.[2]

Tradition that extends from the Mediterranean classical into the post-classical northern European world and helps to form the medieval grotesque, especially that in manuscript illumination, is to be found in the decorative convention known as the inhabited scroll and in conventions related to it.

---

[1] On grylles see Jurgis Baltrusaitis, *Le Moyen Âge fantastique: antiquités et exotismes dans l'art gothique*, Paris, 1955, pp. 13 ff.

[2] Ernest Kitzinger, *Early Medieval Art in the British Museum*, 2nd edn., London, 1955, p. 10.

The vine- or leaf-scroll in the late classical world is an ornament that may be used with or without contained figures, which may be animals, or human beings, or both. Its branches of vegetation may be so designed as to form a regular series of open spaces, tending to be circular, within which the figures may be placed. Or, when there is no series of regular spaces, the figures may be placed within casually formed interstices of the spreading branches. Where there is action it may be as simple as a running or leaping animal in each of a series of circles.[1] Or the action may constitute a scene with a touch of the dramatic. Where it does, a favourite subject is the pagan Bacchic vintage, which early Christianity adapts to its use because of original religious symbolism found in the vine and in the wine from its grapes.[2] An example of such Christian adaptation is in the mausoleum at Rome built by Constantia, daughter of Constantine, between 337 and 350.[3] A mosaic in the vaulting of the gallery shows a spreading vine. Between its branches and around it the vintage is carried on by wingless cupids, who in Roman decoration seem to have become interchangeable with cupids bearing wings and who in the Renaissance came to be called *putti*.[4] These pagan figures of love, now put into service in the interests of Christian love, climb upon the branches to gather grapes in baskets, while birds perch on branches or fly among them. In the centre the vine forms a circular space. Within this there is a human portrait, which thus becomes a bit of non-grotesque delineation framed by a generous grotesque design. At two opposite sides of the area covered by the vine the action that begins in the vine is carried to completion. Here *putti* driving ox carts bring in the harvest and other *putti* crush the grapes with their

[1] As, for example, in the leaf-scroll design from the fifth century reproduced in John Beckwith, *Coptic Sculpture: 300–1300*, London, 1963, Plate 76.

[2] See, for example, Erwin R. Goodenough, *Jewish Symbols in the Greco-Roman Period* (Bollingen Series xxxvii), New York, 1956, vi. 46–53.

[3] Reproduced in F. van der Meer and Christine Mohrmann, *Atlas of the Early Christian World*, trans. and ed. Mary F. Hedlund and H. H. Rowley, London, 1958, p. 63, Plate 137.

[4] On such figures as being interchangeable see Erwin R. Goodenough, op. cit., vi. 50.

feet. Another example of such Christianizing of pagan grotesque figures is on a sarcophagus of the end of the third century in the Museo Lateranense at Rome.[1] Here the scene has been given greater scope. It develops a pastoral theme as well as the theme of the vintage. The space on one side of the sarcophagus is tightly filled with a background of spreading vines, and among their branches not only do cupids climb to harvest grapes (winged cupids in this instance) and birds perch, but also at one side Eros is seated and Psyche offers grapes to her love. On the ground beneath the vine cupids carry out other stages of the vintage and act the shepherd's part by showing tender care for lambs and by milking. Standing on pedestals before the vine are three human figures, each with a sheep upon his shoulders, who are presented in the tradition of Christ the Good Shepherd, rescuer of lost sheep and protector of the flock.[2]

Related to regularized spaces in classic grotesque design that are formed by branches of vegetation are those formed by more abstract means. At their simplest they result from a loose continuous twisting or interlacing of two narrow strips, with one strip rising to form the upper half of a circle and the other descending to form the lower half and with each strip going first behind the other and then in front. In a succession of circles like this on a wood frieze of the fifth or sixth century (from a monastery of Upper Egypt, and now at Berlin in the Staatliche Museen) one finds, for example, winged cupids, birds, and human portraits.[3] The interlacing that creates such circles can be followed by the eye with ease, but interlacing becomes tighter and more complicated in classical plait-work used for geometric borders. Yet in interlacing, whether in a vegetation design or in one of abstract lines, the classical decorative art never fails to show something of a restraint that the medieval decorative art disdains, in interlacing as in other matters.

[1] Reproduced in F. van der Meer and Christine Mohrmann, op. cit., p. 44, Plate 67.

[2] A brief account of this convention in its relation to its pagan background is in Michael Gough, *The Early Christians*, London, 1961, pp. 90–2.

[3] Reproduced in John Beckwith, op. cit., Plate 48.

Though such restraint is unmistakable in the inhabited scroll of the kinds so far considered, yet fantasy is at work there, and where it works upon nature it reshapes it for a purpose, with the result that there is what may be called mild deformation. This is done often in a low-keyed spirit of gaiety. There is action, but violent contentions seem not to be called for. Nor is monstrosity a theme.

But monstrosity is very definitely a theme in the type of Roman decorative wall painting which is most familiar in discoveries made at Pompeii. This is the decoration, whether found at Pompeii or in Roman ruins elsewhere, which is supposed to have brought two terms into existence in the Renaissance: 'grotesque' (the French form of the Italian adjective *grottesca*, from *grotta*, i.e. grotto, as apparently used to mean the buried chamber of an ancient building) and 'antic' (the English form of the Italian adjective *antico* or *antica*, as apparently used to mean grotesque and to characterize the fantastic spirit of ancient ornamental paintings found in the discovered 'grottoes').

An example of decoration on the wall of a room may be offered to show how the Pompeian art of perspective in wall painting, fancifully extending space beyond the boundaries of the room, may employ panels that contain framed scenes or portraits surrounded by grotesque borders in which deformation of nature produces monstrosity.[1] In this example a central panel of three presents non-grotesquely a mythological scene within a rectangular frame. Around the framed scene, taking up more space on the panel than the scene, is a grotesque border that is mainly of vegetation-like scroll-work. This departs from nature not only in its formalization but also in its incorporation of human figures, some of them winged, which tend to merge at their heads and feet with the scroll and to become sections of it. Birds perch on the scroll. At the bottom of it are two goats. In a shallow section of the panel below the scroll is a scene in which three winged cupids engage in a spirited chariot race driving goats. Between the central panel and the ones on either side of it are painted narrow

[1] Reproduced in Ludwig Curtius, *Die Wandmalerei Pompejis: eine Einführung in ihr Verständnis*, Leipzig, 1929, p. 175, Plate 108.

perspectives leading the eye away from the room and off down a line of high columns and galleries. In each side panel is a circle containing portraits which is surrounded by a grotesque border comparable to that surrounding the mythological scene in the central panel. In a shallow lower section of each side panel is a hunting scene, one being of dogs pursuing a deer and the other of dogs attacking a wild boar. Above and below these panels are grotesques that include griffin-like figures and also sea-monsters, one of them part man. In the hunting scenes there is representation of combat, but this is a very minor matter. What dominates is a profusion of delicacy in grotesque imagination which may strike one as being unduly fine-spun.

The delicate monstrosities produced in such classic decoration when human, animal, or bird figures undergo partial change into vegetation or something similar are highly varied. Human beings or cupids may fray out at the legs or arms into branches of vegetation bearing leaves or into abstract curves that suggest vegetation. So too may the hinder parts of four-footed beasts be transformed.[1]

There are somewhat comparable transformations to be found in the medieval grotesque, but it was the Renaissance that brought a close following of classic tradition in grotesque creations of this order. Among many Renaissance examples are those that occur within decorative borders used by Elizabethan printers and publishers for title-pages of books.[2] (For one such border see the illustration facing page 38.) Much adaptation of classic grotesque decoration in general is to be found in these title-page borders and also in the ornamental devices used by Elizabethan printers and publishers to distinguish their productions from those of others.[3] But in such adaptation, even where classical inspiration is strong,

---

[1] Reproductions of a varied lot of figures thus transformed are in H. G. Beyen, *Die pompejanische Wanddekoration vom Zweiten bis zum Vierten Stil*, i, *Tafeln*, Haag, 1938, p. 53, Plate 200; ii, *Tafeln*, Haag, 1960, p. 54, Plate 139; p. 57, Plate 139; p. 59, Plate 207; p. 67, Plate 232; p. 80, Plate 269.

[2] As shown in R. B. McKerrow and F. S. Ferguson, *Titlepage Borders Used in England & Scotland, 1485–1640*, London, 1932.

[3] As shown in R. B. McKerrow, *Printers' & Publishers' Devices in England & Scotland, 1485–1640)*, London, 1913.

there may be the reminder that the Renaissance can show itself as an extension of the Middle Ages. The informing spirit within a grotesque border or device may change suddenly and surprisingly from classical to medieval.

It happens that Nicholas Ling, the publisher of both the 1603 'bad' quarto and the 1604–5 'good' quarto of *Hamlet*, used a device on the title-page of each of these editions which provides an example of such change in spirit. Ling used the device also on the title-page of Thomas Nashe's *Pierce Pennilesse his Supplication to the Diuell* in 1595 and on that of Henry Smith's *Three Sermons* in 1607. We may presume that it was made to suit his own fancy as well as the fancy of the man who designed it. He had his initials worked into it. The fact that in its particular way it says something about taste for the grotesque in Elizabethan England is important, not the fact that it came to be attached to quartos of *Hamlet*. At the centre of the device is a honeysuckle design with flowers and leaves and with a fish entangled in tendrils. Obviously, the fish, as a ling, is meant to be a rebus on Ling's name. The honeysuckle branches are supported from below by two wingless cupids, or *putti*, that help to form the base of the border. They are seated upon the curved, closed ends of classically fanciful cornucopias, which tend to fray slightly into vegetation offshoots as they broaden toward their openings to begin forming the sides of the border. At the base of the border and the lower parts of its sides classical tradition is honoured fairly well, notably in a lion-like human face between the curled lower cornucopia ends, which is somewhat similar to a figure used architecturally as a rainspout on the roof of a classic temple, but is very different in spirit of presentation from a medieval gargoyle on a cathedral. Yet, as the sides of the border ascend, the quality of it changes sharply. Issuing from the mouths of the cornucopias are not only the fruits to be expected, but also growing branches of vegetation from which on each side of the border a monster in dragon form is disentangling its long serpent tail as it is urged upward by a riding winged cupid. Each dragon's head is turned viciously toward its rider and appears to threaten resistance to being urged onward. The urging seems to drive the two dragons toward a meeting in combat at the top of the device. A monstrous figure in keystone position at the top has incompletely a woman's body and on this a beast-like or owl-like head. This figure reaches out with a hand on either side to draw the riders onward and to bring the dragons together for their apparently destined encounter.

The theme here of violent struggle engaged in by human beings and by animals or monsters, within and against an entanglement in the form of vegetation, is a characteristic one in the medieval grotesque. It is markedly different from the theme of such figures at rest or in generally undisturbed action, with a vegetation form merely framing them or even supporting them, which is an equally characteristic theme of the classical grotesque. The theme of tension in monstrosity to match that of violence in struggle, often enough with an ominousness such as that expressed in the concept of the dragon, is likewise characteristic of the medieval grotesque, particularly in its earlier stages. The classical monster is usually mild by comparison.

Something further should now be said about the spirit that distinguishes the medieval grotesque from the classical. I have mentioned the decorative spout that serves to conduct rain-water from a classic temple roof as being different from the decorative spout that serves a like purpose on a medieval cathedral. The difference between them is a measure of distance between corresponding realms of the imagination. Fancy forms both. Nevertheless, the gargoyle on the cathedral is frequently given fantastic qualities not to be found in its counterpart on the temple, which in its favoured form is simply, and even rather nobly, a lion's head. A somewhat closer correspondence with the spirit of the gargoyle can at times be found in a distorted human face or a gorgon face on an upright terracotta antefix used to conceal an open tile end on the temple roof.[1] But the gargoyle tends far more to depart monstrously from representation of normal forms of life and of anything that can be

---

[1] The imaginative range of the antefix is well presented by illustrations in the article 'Antefissa' in the *Enciclopedia dell'Arte Antica Classica e Orientale*, Rome, 1958, i. 404–7.

called nobility. It departs farthest when it becomes something with compound form, such, for example, as a fool mounted upon the shoulders of a presumedly wise old man the better to spew water away from a building. It then is monstrous by having oppositions within itself as well as by being opposed without to the cathedral sacredness to which it is joined. Its monstrosity always produces strain or struggle that is essentially dramatic.[1]

From its beginnings the medieval grotesque spirit offers rudimentary drama in the oppositions it brings into being. In England as early as the beginning of the eighth century it uses in the illumination of a well-known Christian manuscript a style of northern pagan decoration in which there is the theme of violent animal struggle, and it allows with seeming delight and with undeniably beautiful effect an over-all conflict between this and the matter it decorates. The manuscript is that of the Lindisfarne Gospels. The style of decoration is closely related to that of some of the Anglo-Saxon metal work, of admirable skill, found on secular objects discovered when the mid seventh-century ship burial at Sutton Hoo in East Anglia was excavated in 1939. Where the theme of animal struggle appears in the Sutton Hoo metal-work or in the Lindisfarne Manuscript decoration, its dramatic action tends at first glance to become lost in a scheme of larger geometrical design. It does so particularly in the Lindisfarne Manuscript decoration, where there is much purely abstract interlacement of lines. But here the eye is soon enough drawn to an interlacement of creatures with elongated snake-like flexible bodies and with fiercely biting or fiercely threatening mouths. The heads are sometimes bird-like, with beaks, and sometimes beast-like, with snouts and ears. The biting is often done upon a surrounding tangle of vine-like loops. In addition to entangled creatures with snake-like bodies there are some with bird bodies as well as bird heads.

In the Gospel Book of Durrow, earlier by perhaps half a century, a grotesque art that has been called Hiberno-Saxon produces

---

[1] The imaginative range of the gargoyle, in both simple and compound forms, is equally well presented by illustrations in L. B. Bridaham, *Gargoyles, Chimères, and the Grotesque in French Gothic Sculpture*, New York, 1930, pp. 23–61.

on one page, which is completely filled with ornamental patterns, a similar design of animal action. This page faces the page of text that opens the Gospel of John. Even more quickly than any page in the Lindisfarne Gospels it draws the eye away from a geometrical over-pattern to a living motion of entwined and struggling creatures within a framed space. Moreover, the motion is more violent. It is filled with conflict, not only that which creature can have with creature or creature with environment, but also that which the creature can have with itself. Creatures bite and hold each other and also bite and hold parts of themselves in order to form looped patterns. Some have snake-like bodies monstrously provided with legs and some have more naturally beast-like bodies, but all have beak-like jaws.

As Margaret Rickert aptly says, these 'bands of elongated biting animals (so-called lacertines) seem to be all of one breed', whatever the variation in them.[1] It may be added that theirs is a breed which produces a host of striving and straining figures in the later medieval grotesque, including the elongated gargoyle with its many animal and human forms.

3

It is when the medieval grotesque becomes Gothic that it brings comedy into religious art—comedy, that is to say, about which there can be no doubt as to its being consciously achieved by the artist. At whatever point one thinks of Gothic art as truly beginning, one recognizes that by the thirteenth century it is to be found in being. The grotesque comedy that has appeared by then is very much of the kind that we call low comedy when we find it in medieval drama of a later time and in Renaissance English drama. The clash of such comedy with the guiding high seriousness of medieval religious art, whether in church structures, manuscripts, or plays, may appear to be greater than its clash with what we count its opposite in the plays of Shakespeare and in the

---

[1] Margaret Rickert, *Painting in Britain: The Middle Ages*, London, 1954, p. 11.

Elizabethan drama generally, though the clash in Shakespeare is great enough to make us highly sensitive to it. We sometimes wonder that the Gothic medieval man seems to be little sensitive to the clash as it exists in art around him.

The Gothic spirit of comedy that begins to work within medieval fantasy is not one to transform utterly the Romanesque grimness and ominousness given to the grotesque. In the medieval drama and also in the Shakespearean the Gothic grotesque may show something of these Romanesque qualities along with comic qualities. Near the beginning of the thirteenth century there is an aesthetic revolution, but at the same time a certain amount of an informing older spirit strongly survives. As Lawrence Stone observes: 'The popularity of the twelfth-century theme of the human being struggling amid enveloping coils of foliage containing monstrous beasts is surely of more than purely stylistic significance.'[1] For, as he goes on to say, with the coming of the thirteenth century this theme of man's struggle continues, however much man changes his vision of the struggle.

How difficult it is to be sure whether humour exists in the medieval grotesque before the end of the twelfth century may be realized if one looks closely at a variety of scenes found in ornamentation applied to church treasures of north-western Europe. Among them are scenes presenting such things as these: men working upward through tangled scrolls (tenth century); men forcing their way through a tangled vine, one eating grapes from it (eleventh century); figures in scrolls formed by a conventionalized vine, these figures being a leaping goat, a leaping dog apparently pursuing the goat, a striving man badly entangled and pierced through the chest by one of the branches of the vine, a bird of prey entangled by and biting the vine, another bird of prey entangled and doing the same, a man gripping a branch and working through the tangle (eleventh century); a man entangled in a leafy scroll, climbing and forcing a sword down the mouth of a dragon pressing after him from below (twelfth century); an ape attacked

[1] Lawrence Stone, *Sculpture in Britain: The Middle Ages*, Harmondsworth, 1955, p. 107.

by two dragons, one on either side, the struggling figures being tangled in a scroll (twelfth century).[1]

Of these scenes the one that has most suggestion of humour is the last, which was conceived later than the others, *c.* 1183. But the ape appears terrified, and if there is humour here, it is not without harshness. The fact that it is an ape and not a man that suffers the attack is in itself a suggestion of humour, for with the coming of comedy into the Gothic grotesque the ape quickly becomes established as a comic figure in the close and apparently indecent likeness to man that he shows on the animal plane. In Gothic marginal grotesques on manuscript pages he has been found to play a more conspicuous comic part than any other animal.[2]

If there is humour elsewhere in the scenes just described, it exists somewhat uneasily. Perhaps the incident of the man pulling grapes to eat in the midst of a painful struggle that might well take his whole attention offers a certain comic incongruity, but probably it offers only grimness, including that of hunger. The Romanesque theme of man striving as he does here within a tangled mass seems always to have some grimness. It often seems to take on a special grimness when the striver is naked—when he is the poor, bare, forked animal to which Shakespeare makes King Lear reduce himself.

Comedy in medieval manuscript illumination takes on form and substance more and more clearly as grotesque ornament breaks free from confinement within initials and spills over into page margins. In England it appears in a form especially noteworthy in psalters of the latter part of the thirteenth century and the early part of the fourteenth. These have significance not only for the splendour of their illumination in general but also for the vigour in their comic presentation of figures in action within marginal ornament. This vigour has its part in a development of the grotesque spirit that asks with some insistence to be called English.

[1] For all of these scenes see illustrations in Hanns Swarzenski, *The Monuments of Romanesque Art: The Art of Church Treasures in Northwestern Europe*, London, 1954, Figures 111, 159, 160, 205, 531.

[2] See H. W. Janson, *Apes and Ape Lore in the Middle Ages and the Renaissance*, London, 1952, p. 164.

The development of that spirit in Elizabethan drama is much more advanced but of the same order. It, too, asks to be called English, with even greater insistence.

Such marginal illumination of psalter pages, it is always to be remembered, is decoration of a revered religious text, and where it is comic it can only be taken as something of low order joined to something of high order. As a reminder of the truth of its lowness there is in it often enough the theme of the low being made high, but made so in presumptuous violation of all natural possibility and therefore in a grotesquely incongruous manner that brings laughter. The theme presents a topsy-turviness where the down in a hierarchy becomes the up. It offers incidents in which the timid rabbit is like the worm that turns. He hunts the dog, or beats the dog, or leads a bear captive. In one incident a triumphant upright-walking rabbit returns from the chase, blowing a hunting horn and carrying as trophies two dead dogs hung head down from a pole over his shoulder. In another a rabbit makes a clean hit with an arrow shot at a fleeing dog.[1] In the same way an incident in which mice hang a cat is part of the theme.[2]

In the Gothic drolleries upon manuscript page margins the ape also has a presumption that makes his low comically into high. But he is not a worm that turns. In nature he is not of the most humble degree in the hierarchy of life, but is all too challengingly and unashamedly close to man. Hence the grotesqueness of the ape seen in comparison with man is always of the so-near-and-yet-so-far variety. It is such when, for example, a Gothic drollery makes him into a knight bearing a lance, but wearing the ape countenance still and contenting himself with a pig for his mount. There is a like effect when the incomplete transformation is into a nobleman mounted upon a goat and gloved for hawking, but holding upon his right hand a lowly bird of prey, the owl, which with a pointing left hand he is severely commanding to fly at some

---

[1] For incidents in which the rabbit thus becomes a conqueror see S. C. Cockerell, *The Gorleston Psalter: A Manuscript of the Beginning of the Fourteenth Century*, London, 1907, p. 28 and Plate X.

[2] See Joan Evans, *English Art: 1307–1461*, Oxford, 1949, p. 9.

object of the hunt. The theme of apes made into fantastically mounted noblemen and giving themselves to owling instead of hawking was a popular one.[1]

One may be sure, then, that grotesque comedy is offered here in the figure of the ape seen as imperfectly a cavalier. May one take it that grotesque comedy is also offered here in the figure of the cavalier seen as unjustifiably elevated among men? It does not seem so. It does not seem that what can properly be called social satire is present. Nor does it seem that satire is present which lashes particular human follies—hawking viewed as a folly, for example. But one may say with good reason, judging from the larger Gothic theme of animals grotesquely acting human parts, that there is here the implication, call it satirical if one will, that man in general, in all the pride he takes in his humanity, is foolish enough to need the ape as a particularly shocking reminder that he is animal as well as something more. The reminder, then, is for Everyman, not merely for the nobleman, the man on horseback. The warrior noble, proud of mastering his hawk because it is a bird admired for having a nobility of its own in the way of an achieved domination, can stand especially well for pride in all men. When an ape holding on his wrist an ignoble owl, a bird that can even prey upon mice, is shown acting with successful presumption the part of the nobleman, then the medieval man of any sort may well be shaken by the spectacle. If the high and mighty man can thus be taken down in his human pride, it is all the plainer that mankind in general can be. Man can think of himself still as being elevated above the beast, but yet, when he can see a so-near-and-yet-so-far grotesqueness in the ape in relation to himself, he can also see a so-far-and-yet-so-near grotesqueness in himself in relation to the ape. He can add a dimension to his knowledge that he is animal as well as man.

At this stage, as is plentifully revealed in Gothic art, man shows marked capacity to be a laughing animal. He can laugh not merely

---

[1] For such scenes, including those here described, see H. W. Janson, op. cit., illustrations following Chapter VI ('The Ape in Gothic Marginal Art'), Plates XXIII to XXVI.

at animals put into human form but also, in the way of greater
achievement, at himself put into animal form. He does both
of these things in his creation of adventures for Reynard the
Fox as well as in grotesque creations such as we have been
considering.

What he thus creates has a share in the medieval onslaught
against pride as a deadly sin, but it seems to be in essence a thing
of easy enjoyment. It seems to come from a gaiety that spon-
taneously follows a path somehow opened to it by forms of
thought and art in earlier medieval centuries that did not appear
to be inviting gaiety. To ask how gaiety could thus all at once
come strongly into the medieval presentation of man in relation
to a natural world of entangling tendrils and of struggling beasts
and monsters, a theme that had long been marked by little if anything but ominousness and foreboding, is perhaps to ask an un-
answerable question about how culture comes to be shaped by men,
and men in turn come to be shaped by culture.

At the same time that gaiety comes into the marginal grotesques
of manuscript illumination, realism begins to show itself among
them. A delight taken in the depiction of the natural simply for its
natural quality is now so close to the gaiety with which the grotesquely unnatural can be depicted that a curious community of
spirit may be sensed here between what is undoubtedly realism
as we have grown accustomed to use the term and what is very
much an opposite of this. Quite obviously the joining in spirit
takes place because of an adventurous playfulness in both. In one
mood this playfulness explores the world and records with truth
to its natural forms a variety of things observed, but in another
mood it declares a freedom to depart from the restraints of such
recording and to explore ways of reshaping nature fantastically.
In play the realistic and the fantastic are often mixed or blended.
There may be animals and branches of vegetation presented as
they are found in nature, and on the same page there may be presented vegetation that is abstractly stylized, animals that act men's
parts, and monsters that never were. An animal acting a man's
part may be created by a mild fancy and be only a pig that is

wholly pig except for the fact that it is fiddling, or playing a harp, or blowing a trumpet. Then again it may have about it much more of the drama of presumption, like the mounted ape acting the hawking nobleman.

When comedy and realism enter the medieval grotesque, they do not completely conquer the forbidding imaginative quality that we have found to be characteristic of it for centuries. Indeed, something of this forbidding quality remains to carry over into the Renaissance grotesque. It is strongest, of course, where the Renaissance grotesque has most of the medieval temper, and weakest where the grotesque consciously turns back toward the classical grotesque. In the Shakespearean grotesque, as we shall find, it is always waiting to show itself.

The Luttrell Psalter comes late (*c.* 1340) among the celebrated psalters illuminated in the neighbourhood of East Anglia. Its decorations include many realistic scenes in which English life on the everyday plane is pictured simply for its ordinariness. Among them are kitchen or dinner scenes, for example, and scenes in which there is archery practice, or a boy stealing cherries, or a doctor bleeding a patient. Also included are standard animal scenes of Gothic comedy, such as one in which an ape drives horses hitched to a cart. Yet on almost every page it has grotesques that are extraordinary for the way they carry the figuration of monstrosity to a forbidding extreme which has been called 'nightmare-like'.[1] In these there is much combat and much threatening expression of countenance. There is also much complicated deformity, like that in a figure with an ox's head, a body somewhat like an alligator's, and a pair of human legs curiously spotted. Realism and comedy, as interlopers in the grotesque, seem here to have forced monstrous fantasy into taking violent forms in order to prove its continued presence. But realism and comedy are interlopers in the medieval grotesque only for a brief while. They are soon given freedom to range within it.

[1] E. G. Millar, *The Luttrell Psalter: Two Plates in Colour and One Hundred and Eighty-three in Monochrome from the Additional Manuscript 42130 in the British Museum, with Introduction*, London, 1932, p. 15.

4

Opposition of the grotesque to matter of avowed elevation to which it is attached is clear throughout the Middle Ages and on into the English Renaissance. Yet in Shakespeare the grotesque shows that it has acquired an ability to join with such matter in ways that make for the two a bond of substance if not a union in spirit. It has often been remarked that the earlier medieval grotesque may be found to have little relevance as an accompaniment of what it decorates. Before it becomes part of drama its indications of relevance are indeed few and often unclear, whether its decoration is applied to the exterior fabric of a church, to capitals, misericords, and other interior parts of a church, to church treasures, or to religious manuscripts. But particularly in manuscript illumination there is a growing tendency for these indications to show themselves and to become clearer. This comes most noticeably at the time that comedy and realism are growing within the grotesque.

Even at the close of the Romanesque period designs may now and then be found in which there appears to be hesitant probing for capabilities of relevance in the grotesque that are fully to reveal themselves later. One may with justification think that there is some probing of this kind in the illumination of MSS. Auct. E. infra 1–2 in the Bodleian Library, in which there are no marginal grotesques but many finely executed grotesque initials. The two manuscripts form a Latin Bible on parchment that was written in England in the latter half of the twelfth century. From its initial designs I choose two for special consideration. It should be understood that among the initials of this Bible these are unusual in the extent to which they suggest grotesque relevance.

The first of them is at the beginning of Genesis and is the 'I' of *In principio*.[1] It is a narrow elongated design with Christ at the top presented as Creator of the world. Immediately below the figure of Christ there are some involved loops in abstract form. Entwined in these loops are the arms of a man who suspends himself from

[1] MS. Auct. E. infra 1, fol. 6ᵛ.

them. His long thin body fully clothed in a robe (not naked as that of a man entangled in a grotesque involution often is) hangs above an array of buildings which seem to represent the scene of life on earth. Below these is the coiled grotesque form of a dragon, with a beast's head and a threatening open mouth. The man looks upon the buildings below and the dragon beneath them with a startled open-mouthed expression. It may well be one of horror. The figure of Christ has relevance, of course, to the religious matter which the design decorates. What the grotesque figures in the rest of the design may be taken to be is a challenging question. They could have something to do with the drama of man in the world that results from the events chronicled in Genesis.

The design as a whole certainly suggests relevance. It troubles us by suggesting relevance incompletely but temptingly. There is a very possible implication that the suspended man is supported by God in Christ, to whom he desperately holds, as he looks down in dismay at what the world now is, not in its created state but in a state resulting from the Fall. Part of such an implication would be given by the dragon coiled at the base of the world, which, according to a long and well established tradition, could symbolize Satan. Here it would be the Satan responsible for the Fall, who is now at home on earth and is always lying in wait for man. The suspended man, then, would be in danger of losing his precarious hold upon what is above him and of dropping down to that which is quite understandably capable of horrifying him as he gazes at it. This grotesque design presents something that is common enough in other grotesques of the Romanesque period, namely the perturbation of a man grasping loops of an involution and threatened by one or more monstrous figures near him. But here there is a difference in the use of the theme. This man apparently strives to find safety by holding to coils of divine support instead of striving to escape from entanglement in coils of the natural world, as other men appear often to be doing in a Romanesque grotesque design. One thing more should be said about this man and his setting. There is nothing humorous to be seen in his presentation, which has the full Romanesque austerity though it is late Romanesque.

The second grotesque design from this manuscript which I think deserves special consideration is the initial to the Book of Job.[1] (See the frontispiece of this book.) Here we have a design made to accompany a narrative of human suffering that invites comparison with outstanding dramatic tragedies. The question of its relevance claims attention as we approach the Shakespearean grotesque and the bearing upon tragedy that this comes to have.

In the design the 'V' in the word 'Vir' at the beginning of Job (*Vir erat in terra Hus nomine Iob*) is formed by the head and body of a dragon. The head of the dragon is not a typical one in grotesque design of the period. The dragon in any form may, according to tradition, be a symbol for Satan, but here, instead of the usual beast head, it has a human head, and this is given a regal appearance that is emphasized by fanciful indication of a crown. There seems thus to be some suggestion of the Prince of Darkness, of the Satan who has been given leave by God to assail Job with suffering and temptation and who is the enemy of all mankind. A notable feature of the dragon's head is the projection from its side that asks to be taken as either the horn of a beast or the ear of a beast, but demands no decision as to which, since the suggestion of bestial devilishness added to regality is the same either way.

The snake-like body of the dragon curves downward from the head on the right and then upward on the left to make the letter 'V'. It forks on its upward course to produce coils that complete the outline of the letter and other coils that fill the space within the letter. Both sets of coils produce typical involutions of medieval grotesque design. Both take on the character of the foliate scroll by fraying out into sprout-like growths and producing the common grotesque monstrosity of animal-like or man-like substance that can also be plant-like substance. Within the central coils there is a typical naked man entangled after the Romanesque style. He is typically accompanied by threatening creatures likewise entangled.

The typicality of the man gets in one's way if one tries to make him a representation of Job himself in the toils of his suffering.

[1] MS. Auct. E. infra 1, fol. 304[r].

One may do better to think of him as an ordinary and less indi-
vidualized man who has been involved before in the thicket of the
world in many similar designs, and who therefore comes easily to
the mind and hand of the artist when the design for the Book of
Job is needed. The encircling and dominating form of the dragon
seems to spread its coils, then, throughout the world and to reach
beyond Job to entangle the ordinary man, who becomes a figure
of mankind. But the ordinary man pushing his way through im-
peding coils seems here not merely to show strain and perturbation, as he often does. He is stretching an exploring hand toward
the dragon's head and has an open-mouthed expression that reveals more curiosity than dismay. Is this naked and defenceless
explorer of evil someone who is comically insensitive to danger
in his action, like the conjuring ostler in Marlowe's *Doctor Faustus*,
who raises Mephistopheles by Faustus's book and is changed into
an ape for his pains? It can only be said that on this point the design
is completely enigmatic, as the Romanesque grotesque commonly
is when there is question as to a possible showing of humour.

In the same manuscript Bible that contains these grotesque
initials to Genesis and Job there is a historiated Beatus initial to the
Psalms that has a spirit not dominantly grotesque.[1] Its 'B' for the
Beatus vir at the opening of Psalm 1 is outlined with some use of
the grotesque foliate scroll, but this is a very minor part of the
design. What is within the outline of its letter may serve well as
the starting-point for a consideration of some significant changes
in the form and spirit of the traditional Beatus initial as it is passed
on in Romanesque and Gothic manuscript illumination. Within
the letter in this case are two straightforwardly representational
pictures of David, of a relevance and a seriousness not to be ques-
tioned so far as David himself is concerned. He is presented in the
lower loop of the 'B' as playing the harp and in the upper one as
writing. The seat on which he sits to play the harp provides one
touch of the grotesque within the outlines of the letter. It has legs
with beast claws and has armrests terminating in beast heads that

---

[1] Reproduced in *English Romanesque Illumination*, Preface by T. S. R. Boase,
Bodleian Library, Oxford, 1951, Plate 12.

look up toward David. If the heads on the terminals look up with a 'responsive expression', as has been thought,[1] then we see here a tie between animal grotesquery and serious matter. If they do not quite do that, these heads at least have a place in a development of the tradition of the Beatus initial that later produces such a tie and also produces humour. That there is humour here in the design of the terminals is as difficult to be sure of as that there is humour anywhere else in grotesque designs of the manuscript. But most certainly these grotesque beast heads do not look upon humanity threateningly.

If we turn from this Romanesque Beatus initial to Beatus initials in the justly famous line of English Gothic psalters, we find at the very beginning of the thirteenth century a Beatus page that goes much farther with the tying of the animal grotesque to matter of elevation. This is in the psalter that is Lansdowne MS. 420 in the British Museum.[2] The 'B' at the centre of the design is formed of an abstract foliate scroll and contains no figures. Around this are two frames, one outside the other. Attached at intervals to the inner frame are eight circles, and at intervals to the outer frame six circles. In the outer circles are men of serious mien, one to each circle, and in the inner circles animals, usually one to each. One of the men is David, who has a place in the middle of one side. He is seated and playing the harp. In the inner circle closest to him is an ape seated like David and looking closely at him the better to imitate him. He is attempting to play a stringed instrument, holding it flat on his knees instead of vertically, as David holds the harp. On the other side of the frame and directly across from the harper David and the would-be harper ape are an ape in an inner circle and a man in an outer circle beside him. This ape has a chain attached to him, and the man beside him holds the chain and threatens him with a raised stick while he gives him instruction, presumably in musical performance. The ape is very obviously resentful. In the other inner circles some of the animals play musical instruments. Among these are an ass playing a harp somewhat

[1] T. S. R. Boase, op. cit., p. 9.
[2] The page is reproduced in Margaret Rickert, op. cit., Plate 94 (A).

like David's, a goat playing a stringed instrument with a bow, and a pig playing shepherd's pipes. There is also an animal of doubtful character who is a juggler and is keeping objects in the air, apparently because in his extreme humbleness he can offer only this accomplishment to match the music-playing of others. The marking off of high from low in this design and the echoing of the high by the low need little comment. The humour is broad and plain. One spirit is evident when animals respond humbly to their betters: another when an ape is ungrateful for instruction from a superior that is accompanied by a corrective beating.

On the Beatus page in other psalters are designs in which low echoes high.[1] On a frame around the 'B' the Psalter of Robert de Lindesey, also of the early part of the thirteenth century, shows David playing the harp in one enclosure, ordinary men in other enclosures playing instruments of commoner type, and an ape in still another enclosure being instructed once more by a man with a threatening stick. Two psalters from the first half of the fourteenth century follow in the presentation of such themes. The Peterborough Psalter (*c.* 1310) shows within the 'B' the harper David and around him three figures, one a man playing a stringed instrument with a bow, another a man strumming a stringed instrument decorated with an animal head, and another a crouching dog listening intently to the second man. The Luttrell Psalter (*c.* 1340) has a Beatus page showing the harper David in the upper left corner, within the 'B', and an ordinary man in the upper right corner facing across the page toward David and playing an instrument so ordinary as the bagpipe.

The question may be asked whether there is satire to be found on the Beatus pages I have described. That David is satirized on these pages is of course unthinkable. He is represented as crowned and truly regal and as being inspired. He is a figure of highness in the worldly realm who, when he strikes his harp and sings, follows the leading of a greater highness in the spiritual realm. The human followers around him, and all the animal followers except the ape,

[1] The three designs described in this paragraph are also reproduced in Margaret Rickert, op. cit., Plates 100, 120, and 131 (A).

have every appearance of being his admiring musical echoers to the limits of their lesser abilities, and to be wholly admirable themselves in following him humbly. As for the ape, he is certainly put before us as having vices and follies to be scourged. One may perhaps say that by coming close to man in his qualities he wins the distinction of being treated satirically, but only because he is a subhuman threat to man's position. Man himself escapes whatever can be called satire here.

Man also escapes satire, one may say, on a page of the Luttrell Psalter where an initial 'C' introducing Psalm 97 (A.V. 98) (*Cantate Domino canticum novum*) shows clerks singing sacred songs. There is in the margin a grotesque monster, which in its upper part is a hooded man playing upon pipes and below the waist has two curiously spotted animal legs and a lizard's tail.[1] This figure seems merely to make a monstrous contribution to a musical page without offering any implied derogatory comment.

In grotesque designs of the psalters it does appear that satire is directed occasionally against certain human failings, as when, for example, a cowled monk in an initial is given a dog's head.[2] This kind of thing is seen in marginal grotesques also. But the extent to which psalter illumination lacks satire is striking. It shows much acceptance, reaching as far as greatly joyful acceptance, of the range of life, from creatures most highly gifted to those most slightly gifted and from normal forms to all imaginable deformations.

Among the psalters the joyful acceptance of life extending from high to low and even reaching to monstrosity is arrestingly shown on two pages of the Gorleston Psalter (which is of the first half of the fourteenth century).[3] The joy comes plainly from the conception that the low has ways of echoing the high and making one with it without giving up its difference from the high. On the first of these pages there is an initial 'E' introducing Psalm 80 (A.V. 81) (*Exultate Deo adiutori*). In the upper part of the initial Christ is seated in glory with orb in left hand and with right hand raised in

---

[1] Fol. 174ʳ, reproduced by E. G. Millar, op. cit.

[2] Lansdowne MS. 420, fol. 24ᵛ.

[3] Fols. 107ᵛ and 106ʳ, reproduced by S. C. Cockerell, op. cit., Plates V and VI.

benediction. Surrounding him four angels are engaged in adoration. In the lower part of the initial there are seven robed musicians. The instruments they play are a hand organ, a harp, a trumpet, a viol, a guitar-like instrument, a psaltery, and a tambourine. In the margins of the page there are: a man in ordinary attire, who plays a bagpipe; a monster with an animal head, human arms, two animal legs, and a waving tail, who plays a flute and beats a gong; and another monster, a crowned centaur, who blows a hunting horn and urges an unconcerned dog to follow some undisturbed rabbits, who appear to be shaking with laughter over the situation. Here the range is from highest to lowest, from divinity to monstrosity and from sacred music to monstrous music. But even the musical efforts of monsters appear to be perfectly acceptable.

The second of these pages is likewise a musical page. It has an initial 'C' introducing Psalm 97 (A.V. 98) (*Cantate Domino canticum novum*). The 'C' is divided across into two compartments. In the upper one the scene is the annunciation of Christ's birth to the shepherds, with the angel in the centre. Two shepherds with a shepherdess between them are to the right, one of the shepherds bent low toward the angel and the other blowing a horn. Three sheep are to the left. These look up at the angel with rapt expressions. In a way somewhat startling their faces have been given a human cast. Their features provide echoes of the horn-blowing shepherd's, which are oafish, though expressive of great good will in their possessor as he blows his horn. In the lower part of the 'C' three clerks in copes sing from a long roll. At the bottom of the page, along with two grotesque monsters which are products of purely irrelevant fancy, there is a man playing an organ. Another man, humbly dressed and wearing a hood, is pumping air for the organ and thus has his lowly part in the rejoicing that takes place.

The Gothic grotesque often shows rejoicing truly enough, a rejoicing in perception of a fascinating complexity in life on earth.[1]

---

[1] The range of theme and mood in marginal grotesques of manuscripts for Gothic Europe as a whole is excellently shown by an extensive assembly of reproductions and by an accompanying analysis in Lilian M. C. Randall, *Images in the Margins of Gothic Manuscripts*, Berkeley and Los Angeles, 1966.

Yet at times it shows a conflicting way of looking at the here and now, an otherworldly way persisting from the Romanesque past. When it has this view, one is reminded that even a poet like Chaucer, with all his Gothic power of rejoicing in man's mortal life, can exclaim, in his poem 'Truth',

> Her is non hoom, her nis but wildernesse.

The Romanesque man, with his common grotesque vision of forcing his way, sometimes clothed and armed but often naked and defenceless, through a wild thicket—a wilderness—where he is threatened by vicious beasts and monsters hostile both to him and to each other, can dramatize himself as being in conflict with a world that suffers from conflict within conflict. It can by its nature even cause conflict within him. This theme of conflict within conflict is too strong to be forgotten in the later medieval grotesque. Nor is it forgotten in the Shakespearean grotesque.

In the Gothic illumination of psalters humour has opportunity to seize upon the theme of conflict. It often does so and takes it into courses of free-ranging fancy in marginal drolleries. Like other marginal drolleries, those in which it proceeds thus are by no means always without apparent relevance to serious matter on any particular page. The amount of strife pictured in relevant and irrelevant grotesques is great and is quite obviously not entirely presented out of pure lightheartedness. It reveals some underlying consciousness of life's being in ultimate truth a sufficiently grim battlefield, no matter what fantastic forms its struggles may be allowed to take in the imagination and no matter what amusement these may provide.

Some of these fantastic forms are extreme indeed. I have already spoken of capacity in the low of the medieval grotesque to elevate itself in preposterous opposition to something that has been dominant over it, as when the rabbit becomes a mighty hunter of the dog. By an even less restrained fantasy, much favoured in Gothic marginal illumination, the snail, far down as it is in the line of creation, becomes a highly threatening adversary of man.[1] In the

---

[1] For the favour given to this theme in North French, Flemish, and English

Gorleston Psalter the snail is represented as capable of attacking a knight (several times), attacking a naked man, attacking a boy who is armed with a hatchet, attacking a pelican, fighting an ape, fighting a nondescript (several times), and defiantly confronting a watchman.[1] In Queen Mary's Psalter (written early in the fourteenth century) fantasy goes to the length of presenting two snails, one large and one small, that menace a monstrous knight, who is prepared to defend himself with a lance.[2] The knight is of a half-man form stranger than the centaur's. He is man down to the waist, wearing chain mail. Below the waist he is a dragon with spreading leathery wings and two legs that are those of a lion.

Among the outstandingly handsome pages of the Ormesby Psalter (*c.* 1310) is one on which David is represented in an initial as being anointed king, while in a marginal grotesque nearby a slinger carrying a shield is shown aiming a stone at a large snail with head threateningly raised.[3] Whether this marginal grotesque, occurring among others on the page that are quite surely irrelevant, is placed here because of a linking of David the King with David the youthful slayer of Goliath, and through him with a slinger in a stock encounter with a snail, is a question.

A realistic and quite obviously appropriate marginal scene of David and Goliath is placed at the bottom of the Beatus page in the Tenison Psalter (earlier than 1284).[4] In the initial David the crowned King is playing the harp, and below him David the youth is facing Goliath in combat. The young David is represented as without armour and as being pitifully small, yet holding a stone at the ready in his sling in determined fashion. The giant Goliath

illumination see Lilian M. C. Randall, 'The Snail in Gothic Marginal Warfare', *Speculum*, xxxvii (1962), pp. 358–67. See also Joan Evans, op. cit., pp. 9 ff.

[1] See S. C. Cockerell, op. cit., p. 28.

[2] A reproduction of this grotesque is in Sir George Warner, *Queen Mary's Psalter: Miniatures and Drawings by an English Artist of the 14th Century, Reproduced from Royal MS. 2 B VII in the British Museum*, London, 1912, p. 183.

[3] Fol. 38ʳ, MS. Douce 366, Bodleian Library, Oxford. The page is reproduced in Sydney C. Cockerell and Montague R. James, *Two East Anglian Psalters at the Bodleian Library, Oxford*, Oxford, 1926, Plate VI.

[4] Add. MS. 24686, British Museum, fol. 11ʳ. The page is reproduced in Margaret Rickert, op. cit., Plate 118.

is a medieval knight, wearing chain mail, carrying a sword, and holding a shield and a lance. The artist makes him a comical coward by picturing him as shrinking away, half turned, from his diminutive opponent in terror. The first few pages of the Tenison Psalter carry on in many of their marginal grotesques the theme of conflict introduced thus early. The second page after the one that has the David and Goliath scene shows a realistic buck fighting a traditional dragon, which is winged and two-legged and has a beast-like head.

A ringing of changes on the theme of conflict is achieved in a truly extraordinary series of marginal scenes in Queen Mary's Psalter. They are at the bottoms of successive pages. On the first of these pages there is a scene, heroic and in no way touched by comedy or fantasy, of combat between two mounted and fully armed knights. One of them is a Saracen who is being pierced by the lance of the other. There seems here to be celebration of a Christian triumph. In creating this scene the artist apparently felt the challenge to produce later as many echoes of the knightly encounter as his imagination could raise. On each of the thirty-three following pages there is a combat that looks back to the knightly combat in a more or less obvious way. Among combats that look back most obviously there are: one between a winged and bearded devil and a legless Saracen who is mounted on a bearded bear; one between two legless men mounted on lions; one between a mermaid and a centaur (the centaur being pierced by the mermaid's lance); one between an ape and a rabbit mounted on monstrous steeds; and one between a mounted ape and a Saracen on foot (the Saracen being pierced by the ape's lance). These are amusingly fantastic grotesques, but at times a scene in the series is not of this order and becomes a realistic presentation of fighting animals— two goats, or a goat and a deer, or two cocks, or two fish.[1] Then the echo of heroic struggle on the human battlefield is found not in a monstrously extraordinary realm but in a realm of most ordinary animality.

[1] Reproductions of scenes in this series are in Sir George Warner, op. cit., pp. 174–82.

A page in the Ormesby Psalter goes so far as to echo in a marginal scene of animality a struggle of such high import as that between good and evil.[1] (See the illustration facing page 32.) In the initial 'D' of the *Dixit Dominus* at the beginning of Psalm 109 (A.V. 110: 'The Lord said unto my Lord, Sit thou at my right hand, until I make thine enemies thy footstool') the illuminator has placed mirror images of God the Father and God the Son. They are seated, the Son to the right of the Father, within an architectural frame representing the Church, and they are flanked by angels. Beneath the footstool on which rest the feet of the Son are prostrate knights in chain mail, who are his enemies ignominiously huddled together in defeat after their struggle against divinity. In the lower border of the page, beneath this historiated initial 'D', is a grotesque design that is dominant within the elaborate offering of marginal decoration surrounding the text. It shows two naked men, one mounted upon a bear and the other upon a lion, fighting savagely with bare hands, catch-as-catch-can. One has the other by the hair, and this other in turn has his opponent by the cheek, with his thumb in the opponent's mouth, undoubtedly being bitten. While the men are thus engaged, their mounts are likewise engaged. The lion has the back of the bear's neck in his jaws and the bear is trying to shake free. The men lean forward to do their fighting over the heads of the fighting animals. Thus on a lower plane, where man challenges man and animal challenges animal, there is combat to match that on a higher plane, where prideful human evil challenges divine good. A conventional winged, two-legged, animal-headed dragon is at either side of this struggle on the lower plane. Neither dragon has a part in it, though one of them views it with interest. Supporting the combatants but not entangling them is a foliate scroll. The combatants have here been granted unhindered action in the natural world. Man in that world, though superior to and the master of the animal he dwells beside, can nevertheless be mastered by the animal he has within him, and can be moved to fight in the naked way of the animal. As he fights thus, impelling the animal at the same time that he is

[1] Fol. 147ᵛ.

impelled by it, he and the animal are grotesque reminders that, as in the realm of being so in the realm of combat, there is a medieval hierarchy reaching from spiritual high to physical low.

5

Comedy in the figuration of the natural world appears in medieval drama at nearly the same time that it appears in many related expressions of the medieval temper. I have been concerned largely with its appearance in English manuscript illumination. Here, it seemed, apart from drama but not unconnected with literature, there was most to show the growth of a spirit which was often distinctly English as well as distinctly medieval and which was capable of producing comedy of a special order in English cycle plays and moralities and later in Elizabethan drama. Chaucer's poetry contains this comedy too, in a form to which D. W. Robertson, Jr. gives rightful place in the medieval grotesque tradition.[1]

Wherever one finds it, this is an order of comedy built upon strong antitheses, both within itself and also between it and matter with which it is associated. The fact that critical discussion of it is often filled with antithetical judgements is not surprising.

We have seen this comedy come into being in a northern European art of grotesque decoration where at first there is a spirit so uncomic as to seem firmly hostile to entrance of the comic, a spirit that finds expression in designs, animate and inanimate, which impute only grimness to the natural world. When the figure of man appears in representations of this world, he is tangled in confused folds of its structure. He must struggle through these while he struggles with beasts and monsters who are also entangled there and are struggling with each other. These other strugglers may even turn fiercely to bite and rend themselves.

This earliest world of the natural in medieval grotesque art may be taken by a later naturalistic age to have about it something that

---

[1] D. W. Robertson, Jr., *A Preface to Chaucer: Studies in Medieval Perspectives*, Princeton, 1962.

Divine Majesty and the Grotesque
A page of the Ormesby Psalter, MS. Douce 366, fol. 147ᵛ; English, *c.* 1310

can only be called strangely 'unnatural'. Like one of its beasts it can turn against itself. It can permit monsters to get into its confines which could not be there by any allowance of occasional deformity or of what we now consider to be natural accident. These are monsters that remind us of those in *Beowulf* and in the northern pagan lore of its background. They are related to the three monsters—Grendel, his dam, and the dragon—which Beowulf conquers in his major epic struggles. Grendel and his dam are flesh and blood, who prey on flesh and blood and can with much difficulty be killed as flesh and blood, but who can at the same time have the qualities of nature spirits that belong to some evil realm of faerie. When they take on the guise of malevolent elves or trolls (beings such as *eotenas ond ylfe ond orcneas*, as the poem calls them in line 112) they are within nature and yet not of that part of nature which helps to produce mankind. Their evil can even be devilish according to Christian conception, though as J. R. R. Tolkien says, in speaking of the shifting of Grendel's qualities from those of an elvish ogre to those of a devil, 'approximation of Grendel to a devil does not mean that there is any confusion as to his habitation', for 'Grendel was a fleshly denizen of this world (until physically slain)'.[1] The winged dragon overcome by Beowulf at the cost of his own life, a dragon like the ubiquitous one we have found in medieval grotesque design, is another monster that is within the natural world, and can be physically killed by man, but approximates evil that is more than natural. Against him man's weapons can be made to work, but in no ordinary way.

With the coming of comedy the monsters remain, but are shaped by an imagination that is in some part an adventurous searching beyond what is fearful in the incongruities that man must encounter. Something of the uncanny departs from monstrosity in a natural world which has an appearance now of growing 'more natural'. As the uncanny lessens in monstrosity there is, not surprisingly, a growing interest in the observed ordinarinesses

---

[1] J. R. R. Tolkien, 'Beowulf: the Monsters and the Critics', *Proceedings of the British Academy*, xxii (1936), p. 283.

of life. There is a 'realistic' use of these by the imagination such as appears in the marginal grotesques of manuscripts along with the fanciful use of monsters. Both uses amuse. Yet they do not always do so. Realistic combats where naked men join beasts in beastliness can at times be depressing to aspiring man. And fanciful monsters like those in the Luttrell Psalter can be nightmarishly unsettling to him.

Thus there comes to be less showing of grimness in the grotesque, but there is always a possibility of its appearance in something like the early form. Grotesque comedy can be unstable in the company of such revived grimness. In drama, as we shall see, it can be unstable indeed where an Iago is the comedian. All comedy has its moments when it is close to becoming or actually does become the opposite of itself, and grotesque comedy most of all.

In drama it is clear, as we have seen it to be clear elsewhere, that medieval grotesque comedy envisages a scale of being in which there is high and low and in which the low, pitted against the honoured high as it is, can show laughable incongruity.[1] It is likewise clear that the low, which in one light is rejectable and sometimes even abhorrently so, is in another light acceptable and sometimes even engagingly so. It is acceptable to the humanity that recognizes lowness in its own shortcomings and yet feels the strange attraction of living with these, no matter how preposterous they are. Thus recognized and accepted with laughter the outrageous low seems to add zest to the recognizing and honouring of the high, which of course could not be honoured at all if there were no low to give it being as an opposite.

The low in medieval drama, as elsewhere in the medieval grotesque, can be incongruously comical simply by being very much itself within a world that honours the high, but it is most comical when it presumes by taking high place. The worm-that-turns, or

---

[1] For a comparison of the comically grotesque low in English mystery plays with that found in various forms of English medieval art see Irena Janicka, *The Comic Elements in the English Mystery Plays against the Cultural Background (Particularly Art)*, Poznań, Poland, 1962.

monde renversé, theme is familiar in the mystery plays and the moralities. When Noah's wife belligerently resists Noah in plays of the Chester, York, and Towneley cycles and in a Newcastle play, she rises defiantly not only against the presumed lord and master who is her husband but also, by implication, against the God who is her husband's lord and whose will is being carried out in the building and using of the ark. Noah's beating of his wife has the comedy of an ordinary incongruity revealed between high and low, but *her* beating of *him* goes beyond that to the comedy of an extraordinary incongruity in a reversal of the accepted order of things, threatened by the low. A threat of reversal somewhat similar is found in the belligerence of the mothers of slaughtered children in the Towneley play on the Massacre of the Innocents. They claw and beat and kick the armed soldiers in the primal way of combat, and lash them with their tongues, but cannot save their children from the sword, much as they disconcert the swordsmen. Grimness in plenty is present here along with low comedy.

But a reversal of the kind thus threatened need not by any means fail to be fully accomplished. In John Pickering's *Horestes* (printed in 1567), where the medieval morality has become what may be called Elizabethan morality-tragedy, a woman armed with nothing but spirited elemental womanhood vanquishes a conventionally armed soldier. The scene is of the briefest, a grotesque piece introduced into the weightier matter of the war of revenge that Horestes is carrying on against Clytemnestra and Egistus. It is like a marginal grotesque moved from outside the text into the text itself. The stage directions reveal its quality. The one at the opening of the scene is: 'Enter a woman lyke a beger rounning before they sodier but let the sodier speke first, but let ye woman crye first pitifulley.' The woman is here seen as in low case indeed, a beggar hunted like an animal by a man who has just killed her husband. She yields, pleading with the 'good master sodier' to have mercy. He says: 'Come followe me.' The stage direction then is: 'Go a fore her, & let her fal downe upõ the & al to be beate him.' The soldier begs for his life and becomes her prisoner. The final stage direction is: 'Take his weapons & let him ryse up

& then go out both.' Grimness is here but suffers in association
with the full-bodied comic reversal.[1]

In a comparable scene of reversal in Thomas Preston's *Cambises*
(printed without date but entered in 1569–70) grimness is so much
overborne by comedy that it almost itself acquires the comic countenance. This play too is a morality-tragedy where warfare has
its echoes on the low comic plane. The scene where woman as the
weaker vessel, the figure of lowness in the world of physical combat, reverses the order of things is that in which Meretrix, a camp-
following prostitute, is the cause of contention for her favours
among three swashbuckling soldiers named Huf, Ruf, and Snuf.
Huf is eliminated because he proves to have no money. Ruf and
Snuf are left and prepare to fight, though Ambidexter, the Vice,
threatens to stop them by turning upon the first one who draws
his sword. At this point a stage direction sketches the beginning
of the reversal: 'Heer draw & fight. Heere she must lay on and
coyle them both, the Vice must run his way for feare, Snuf fling
down his sword and buckler & run his way.' With the Vice and
Snuf gone, Meretrix is able to devote her all to Ruf: 'He falleth
downe, she falleth upon him and beats him, and taketh away his
weapons.' She, not only a mere woman among armed men but
one called whore and shown no respect at all by those who bid
for her, has risen to the top in a particular realm of combat, and
she tells Ruf pointedly how low he has fallen:

> Thou a Souldier and loose thy weapon:
> Goe hence sir boy, say a woman hath thee beaten.

Ruf begs for mercy and she enslaves him. She gives back his sword
and buckler in return for his binding himself to be her ever-
submissive servant 'at place and at boord'. She makes him walk
before her in the way of a gentleman-usher as she leaves for home
where, she is sure, 'customers tarry'.[2]

---

[1] *A Newe Enterlude of Vice Conteyninge, The Historye of Horestes*, ed. Daniel
Seltzer, Malone Society Reprints, Oxford, 1962, ll. 746–75.

[2] *A lamentable Tragedie, mixed full of plesant mirth, containing the life of Cambises
King of Percia*, ed. John S. Farmer, Tudor Facsimile Texts, 1910, sigs. B3–B4.

In this 'lamentable tragedie, mixed full of plesant mirth', as it is characterized on its title-page, the mirth provided by the Vice includes foolery upon the theme of the low that puts itself in high place which had been developed in marginal illumination of manuscripts. At his first entrance the Vice is fantastically armed for war—with a potlid as a buckler and with a rake as a halberd, for example—and the opponents he claims to have readied himself for are creatures of the most harmless lower orders. In the beginning, he says, he is 'appointed to fight against a Snaile'. He thus gives continued life to a favourite illumination drollery. He proceeds to offer more fantasies in kind. The snail vanquished, he must fight a butterfly, and with that vanquished, a fly. Dangerous as these opponents are, he will play the man. As for the fly, he will 'thrust him through the mouth to the knee.'[1] But in manuscript margins this kind of thing had usually come off more amusingly than it does for him.

Just as definite a reminder of the illumination drollery in which the low puts itself in high place occurs in John Skelton's *Magnificence* (c. 1516). The character Fancy, who heads the Vices of the play and helps to bring about the downfall of Magnificence, the King, by turning him away from Measure, is a representative of wanton excess. Fancy has much of the fool about him and says himself that his wits are weak and his brains light. In one scene he enters with an owl on his fist and makes much of it as being a beautiful and talented hawk. He praises it point by point, including its beak. But he is told in scorn that it is well beaked only to catch a rat. Fancy is a version in Vice form of the ape in the manuscript grotesque who makes an owl on his fist into a hawk and thus usurps human nobility.

6

What has just been considered of comedy that issues from presumptuous lowness, and of a contribution made by the Vice to that comedy, leads now to some further consideration of the capacity of evil to take on comic quality in its medieval

[1] Ibid., sig. A4^v.

representation, especially in Gothic drama in England. For evil as pictured and dramatized in the Middle Ages acquires increasingly a comic lowness. It does so as it loses more and more of the respect its fearsomeness first inspired.

We see a part of this change in manuscript illumination when dragons and other monsters, that are uncannily hostile to man in earlier grotesque designs within initial letters, tend later in marginal grotesque designs to give up their uncanniness and become more diverting than threatening. They begin to be mere aberrations of nature, indicating that nature can show curious and amusing imperfections rather than that nature can have an awe-inspiring alliance with forces which are more than natural. Their monstrosity as deformation in nature can eventually fall so low that it can even be counted as being beneath what has the lowness of ordinary or humble form in nature.

We see additional change, usually elsewhere than in manuscript illumination, when infernal devils are given forms that are more and more monstrous after having had early representation as fallen angels with sombre hues but without deformity.[1] They suffer progressive degradation as they are brought down from the realm of evil spirituality into the realm of imperfect nature. They are given bodies formed of human and animal parts, and as the share of animality in these is increased so is their grotesquery. In the eleventh century, for example, the demonic figure may be a bearded old man who is malevolent but has no more of animality about him than writhing serpents upon his head for hair; and in the fourteenth century it may be another bearded old man, likewise malevolent, who instead of serpents on his head has horns, and who, for additional animality, has the claws of a bird of prey in place of feet.[2] The bird claws for feet become for a time

[1] For a tracing of the degradation of Satan in representation see Mâle, op. cit., pp. 370 ff. For a variety of forms given to devils see, among others: Thomas Wright, *A History of Caricature and Grotesque in Literature and Art*, London, 1875, pp. 54 ff.; Henry Charles Lea, *Materials toward a History of Witchcraft*, ed. Arthur C. Howland, 3 vols., Philadelphia, 1939, i. 67 ff.

[2] For the first figure see Margaret Rickert, op. cit., Plate 48 (B); for the second, G. G. Coulton, op. cit., p. 482.

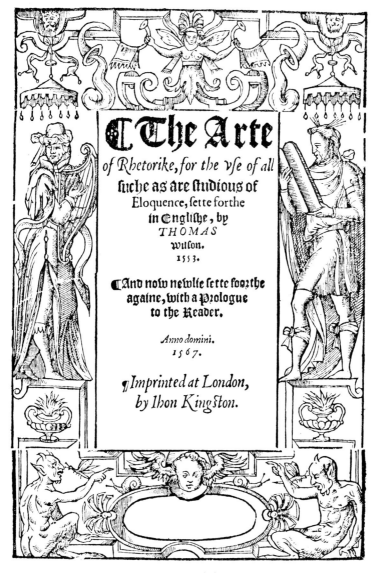

¶ The Arte

of *Rhetorike, for the vse of all*
suche as are studious of
Eloquence, sette forthe
in Englishe, by
THOMAS
wilson.
1553.

¶ And now newlie sette foorthe
againe, with a Prologue
to the Reader.

Anno domini.
1567.

¶ *Imprinted at London,*
by Ihon Kingston.

Divine Inspiration and the Grotesque
Moses and David in a Renaissance title-page border

a favoured convention in devil representation. As devils take on even more fantastically monstrous animal-human form it is plain that, on the medieval stage especially, they come to have a comicality which vies with what remains in them of fearsomeness.

Yet the devils on the stage, as distinct from the Vices, do not come to show a comicality in evil of which much is to be said as preparation for the Shakespearean grotesque. They lack even the rudiments of a quality given in the Shakespearean grotesque to figures that are engagingly unregenerate. In their lowness the devils are comically presumptuous as they continue to wage war against the highness of a ruling divinity, but their presumption is not much more than a roaring and a bellowing. Too often one feels that the dramatist simply makes game of them. It seems that he does so notably when he presents the Harrowing of Hell. They are not often adept devils, either in warring against God or in aping God. But truly enough they are still the Enemy, for man as well as God, and supposedly should not be regarded lightly by man. Man as he welcomed the appearance on the stage of devils that had turned comic may be thought to have laughed at them with a somewhat amiable derision and a simple delight in challenging them to make his flesh creep, but also with a mixture of inherited feelings about the Satanic that were downright uneasy.

But man very clearly did not laugh in that vein as he welcomed the addition of Vices to the company of comic evil on the stage. About the Vice of the morality play as being an unregenerate quality in man that is at work to betray and undo him from within, instead of being a devil that comes against him from without, more will be said in later chapters. It is enough now to make the point that in the Vice medieval man could recognize a part of himself, a portion of fallible nature that had a share in his make-up. This was something very different from the devil that could come from a supernatural realm to take possession of him. One could grant that the Vice, perhaps named Sensuality, or Mischief, or Folly, might of course associate with supernatural evil, might be used by it, and might mischievously take pleasure in getting man into trouble by leading him into evil paths. But, after all, the Vice was not really the Enemy. Nature, to which the Vice belonged, had been corrupted by the Fall and was surely imperfect, but in this life it somehow had its place, within man as well as outside him. It could obviously be enjoyed, though man must always beware of being misled by it. More than that, man could be rather proud of the cleverness of his unregenerate self that he thought he saw in the base shrewdness and vulgar wit of the Vice on the stage. This was not anything to be derided, however loudly it might be laughed at. Its presumption shown against the high was of a different order from that of diabolical presumption, which was as unattractively ridiculous when it bellowed in pride as when it suffered reversal and bellowed in pain.

Much the same comic appeal that the Vice as an abstract figure has in the moralities is also found in some of the concrete figures of lowness in the cycle plays. These at times set themselves against what is above them, even against the highest above them—against God. They do so not because they are essentially or devotedly evil but because a merely human waywardness or perversity is strong in them.

Noah's wife, who is a mild example, can let herself oppose Noah for no good reason when the time comes for her to go aboard the ark. She thus opposes the will of God that acts through a divine command to Noah. But hers is by no means a devilish presumption, though it can be stimulated to action by temptation that comes from a devil. It is even capable of being represented as a natural wifely presumption.

The comicality of a presuming lowness given to Cain the murderer, which is most extensively developed in the Towneley cycle, gives him a position beside Noah's wife, but one in which he much outdoes her. It is remarkable, as has been fully appreciated by critics, how far the Towneley play on the killing of Abel has gone with what may be called Cain's war against God. It makes Cain an egotistic clown and the worst of churls, spoiling for a fight with anyone, from the boy who helps him with his ploughing to the God who expects sacrifice from him and forbids murder. When God speaks to him from above about the rebellious spirit that he

shows as his sacrifice fails to burn, he turns to Abel with the unforgettable lines:

> Whi, who is that hob-ouer-the-wall?
> We! who was that that piped so small?
> Com go we hens, for perels all,
> God is out of hys wit (ll. 297–300).[1]

The still small voice from heaven only convinces Cain that God is
not his friend. He is made firm in that belief when God speaks
again after the murder of Abel. As Cain leaves the scene he calls
down ill upon God because he believes he must now be thrall
world without end to Satan, the foul fiend. Yet we are left with
the feeling that if he ever comes to take the 'stall' in hell that he
expects to have, Satan will rue the day. A man who can be so
outrageous as a foe to God can do at least as well against Satan.
With this thought in mind the medieval spectator could laugh
at him and take a degree of unseemly pride in the stiff-necked in-
transigence of which he shows humanity capable. Cain is a gross
man filled with gross animal combativeness. But anyone who
thinks that he could never find in himself all that makes Cain
boorish may nevertheless be able to recognize some fellowship
with him and to enjoy the shocking relationship. In Cain's case,
as in that of Noah's wife, to be amiably amused at the presumption shown is normal, and to deride it abnormal.

So too for the boy who is Cain's helper. He spoils for a fight as
much as Cain, and together they make a twofold comedy of presumption. The boy is happy to oppose Cain in a way that adds an
echoing sub-plot to the main dramatic action. As Cain presumes
to do battle with and defame the Creator who is over him as lord,
so the boy presumes to do battle with and defame the farmer who
is over him as master. Cain gets a taste of what he inflicts upon
God. In the boy, of course, there is much that looks forward to the
comic presumption of underlings in the Shakespearean grotesque,
most notably that of the overweening clown and the impudent
servant.

[1] What is quoted from the Towneley cycle, here and later, is from the *Towneley
Plays*, ed. George England, E.E.T.S., London, 1897.

The violent presumption of Herod in the English mystery plays, which became a by-word, is greater than Cain's, and moreover, as opposition to divinity, is of very different quality. In what he represents Herod can be supported by Pilate and also by others, such as accusers, torturers, crucifiers, and guards, who are likewise given parts to play as enemies of Christ. In all these, from Herod onward, the ordinary medieval man as spectator is obviously not to find fallible humanity such as he can with amusement see in himself. He is not even to do so by thinking of his own fallibility as similar but milder. For in these there is only humanity that has deserted to join Satan and has left the fellowship of ordinary sinful mankind entirely. Those of this evil company who can be laughed at as fantastic, in the way a boasting and ranting Herod or Pilate certainly can be, may be taken as especially amusing. All can be enjoyed, just as devils are, as good subjects for derision when their actions do not manage to stir too many feelings of uneasiness.

A figure quite unlike any other evildoer in English mystery drama is Mak, in the *Second Shepherds' Play* of the Towneley cycle. He is by no means put beyond human sympathy, though he sometimes seems undeserving of it in that he has a too close relationship with evil that is fiendishly hostile to humanity. He plays the part of a black magician when he draws a circle about the sleeping shepherds to charm them so that he can steal a sheep from them. He has an ill reputation among the shepherds not only as a thief but, in general, as being someone of whom both God and man should beware. When the stolen sheep is discovered in the cradle and Mak's new-born son thus turns out to be a creature with horns, it comes naturally to one of the shepherds to ask Mak what devil (instead of saint) this son of his shall be named after, and to call out to God a warning that Mak has a devilish heir. ('Lo, God, Makys ayre.') In Mak's wife, Gill, there is even the hint of a devil's dam. Yet Mak, though he has an aspect of being dedicated to fiendish evil and thereby possessing a special power, is after all a pitiful underling. He is a starving, poverty-stricken man, and even his presumption can be on a very small scale. He boasts of having high place and a power to compel respect as a yeoman of the King, but he seems to have little hope of being effective with his boasting, and quickly collapses into complaint when he in fact is not effective.

The *Second Shepherds' Play* is remarkable among English mysteries for what it does both in the way of the grotesque and in the way of high seriousness. It well deserves the attention it has had. Those who have written about it in the twentieth century have tended to shift critical concern from the Mak incident to the play as a whole. Truly enough the Mak incident is a praiseworthy piece of plotting skilfully filled out with dialogue, and just by itself it can be thought of as a notable medieval achievement in English comedy. The earlier modern recognition of its achievement includes all due appreciation of the shepherds and of Mak and his wife as being ably characterized after the fashion of an admired realism. It includes little comment on what the whole play comes to as a work of the imagination. One gathers from what earlier comment there is of this kind that the shepherds and the Mak household make up all that is truly outstanding dramatically because they are a product of originality, while the matter in the play drawn from Scripture has come to the dramatist ready-made and resistant to imaginative shaping. One may find in earlier comment such a judgement as the following, which makes the Scriptural matter a briefly developed sub-plot loosely joined to a secular comedy that is really the play: 'The supernatural incidents added to this frank drama of common life have only the slightest thread of connection with the main plot.'[1] In later modern comment it is possible to find criticism maintaining that the play suffers from lack of adequate unification in a way quite different, by having 'cleavage' in it 'between the religious and the secular', which keeps it from showing the 'skilful fusion of drama and doctrine' and the skilful uses of comedy found in mysteries considered to be better.[2] But in general the inclination now seems to be toward praising the play as a whole for uniting its low comedy and

---

[1] Katharine Lee Bates, *The English Religious Drama*, New York, 1893, p. 75.

[2] Eleanor Prosser, *Drama and Religion in the English Mystery Plays: A Re-Evaluation*, Stanford, 1961, pp. 95–6, 186.

its high seriousness. Opinion has even come by stages to see its unity as resulting from something other than a burlesquing or satirizing of the high by the low. It has come to a point where an insistence that this other something is present can be put in terms as emphatic as these: 'To call the Mak story a satire on the Nativity is almost perverse and to call it "a subtle foreshadowing of the scene in the stable", litotes.'[1] One can hardly imagine a judgement like this being passed at the turn of the century.[2]

I take it that there is indeed a close drawing together of high and low in the play. A strong bond that brings the opposing high and low together is the one between the child that is in reality a sheep and the child that is in reality the Lamb of God. Both children can be honoured with gift-giving and be called 'Little Day-Star' by a well-wishing shepherd, and the fact that the first child turns out to be all too simply an animal has grotesque significance in accord with the general importance possessed by the animal theme for the grotesque imagination. The Christ Child is far more than animal, but within the human being which he is there is the animal nature. Concomitantly, as the angel tells the shepherds, this child, of the very highest nobility as the Son of God, lies

> In a cryb full poorely
> Betwyx two bestys (ll. 645–6).

The low shows flagrant presumption by making the household

---

[1] Francis J. Thompson, 'Unity in "The Second Shepherds' Play" ', *Modern Language Notes*, lxiv (1949), p. 306. Thompson comments on the indications that Mak is of the devil's party.

[2] Representative examples of changing opinion on the *Second Shepherds' Play* besides those already cited are to be found in: C. M. Gayley, *Plays of our Forefathers*, New York, 1907, pp. 182–4; Gordon Crosse, *The English Religious Drama*, London, 1913, pp. 65–7; J. B. Moore, *The Comic and the Realistic in English Drama*, Chicago, 1925, pp. 29–35; Millicent Carey, *The Wakefield Group in the Towneley Cycle*, Göttingen, 1930, pp. 190–210; F. T. Wood, 'The Comic Elements in the English Mystery Plays', *Neophilologus*, xxv (1940), pp. 46–7; H. A. Watt, 'The Dramatic Unity of the *Secunda Pastorum*', *Essays and Studies in Honor of Carleton Brown*, New York, 1940, pp. 158–66; A. P. Rossiter, *English Drama from Early Times to the Elizabethans*, London, 1950, pp. 71–2; Irena Janicka, op. cit., 1962, pp. 95–7.

of Mak and Gill offer its grotesque version of what for Yeats in 'The Magi' is

> The uncontrollable mystery on the bestial floor.

It even presumes to make this offering prefigure the event of which it is a version and to let it invite recognition as pointing the way for the coming of that event. But the high stoops to the low to catch up the grotesque and make it part of the mystery. It makes it into more than burlesque prefiguration. It goes so far as to accept Mak's out-of-tune crooning over his sheep-child and transform it with the angelic singing of 'Gloria in Excelsis' at the announcement of the Christ Child's birth.

Beyond matchings of low comedy and high seriousness there is another source of unity in the play. This is an over-all dramatic action that completely absorbs comedy as comedy along with seriousness as seriousness and converts them into the oneness of what may be called a divine comedy. For the play shows men winning through from woe at the beginning to joy in the end as evil is overcome by good. At the beginning each of the shepherds complains of his particular experience of woe in the world. Then the shepherds meet Mak, who seems to be of the devil's party and who certainly is a worker of evil as he adds to their woe by practising guile. They are merciful to him in a Christian comic denouement of the Mak comedy, and merely toss him in a blanket instead of killing him, as they at first have a mind to do. They follow the angel's instructions and seek out the Christ Child, whose coming, one of them says, means that the devil, the false guiler and the causer of woe, has been beguiled. The mother says to them of her child:

> He kepe you fro wo!
> I shall pray hym so (ll. 742–3).

And the shepherds depart, joyfully singing. Mercy has been shown by God to sinning mankind as mercy has been shown by men to a sinning rogue among them. The chief of beguilers, the leader into guile of Mak and other beguilers among men, has been beguiled. A child has come to win back what was lost in Adam's fall. As was foretold, he has come

> to slokyn oure syn
> And slake it,
> Oure kynde from wo (ll. 677–9).

The author of the *Second Shepherds' Play* is not without faults. For one thing he is so much taken with the realistic appeal of ordinary life that his shepherds complain of their woes at greater length than is necessary to make their point, even though the point is in the end to prove important. But the play is one that markedly advances the art of the grotesque in England and looks forward in a way extraordinary for its time to the Shakespearean incorporation of grotesque form with other form.

II

FALSTAFF AND THE MONSTROUS

1

BEFORE Falstaff the Shakespearean grotesque gives promise of producing something like him, but when he appears he is startling in his generous fulfilment of the promise. It is a question whether Shakespeare himself is not startled by what he has conjured up in him, and whether he does not as a result hurry him to his death in *Henry V*, as he gives him only a briefly reported presence off-stage for its accomplishment.

In the two parts of *Henry IV* the presumptuous low within the post-classical grotesque tradition goes for the first time so far beyond being extraneous to the high that it takes a firm stand within the borders of the high and for a time holds a place there. It even has hopes that are not groundless of winning high place there. As Falstaff sets himself to be an apostle of the low and nevertheless indulges such hopes, he trades upon impudence, but by no means upon that alone. He has wit, both for saying and for doing, and this is not the wit of the underling or the boor. Shakespeare has taken pains to put into his background of upbringing the means for him to be in many ways acceptable to the high. It is not for nothing that Justice Shallow speaks of him as having been in boyhood a page to Thomas Mowbray, Duke of Norfolk. Nor is it for nothing that Falstaff has in some way, however devious it might have proved to be if Shakespeare had put it into the picture, gained a knighthood. He is, of course, not to be taken as owing his knighthood solely to Sir John Oldcastle as his prototype. Shakespeare was well able to reject what he did not fancy when working from a source. In short, Falstaff is presented as having had what are called early advantages and as being in that way no merely rude interloper in the realm of the mundane high. More than that, he offers to those of this realm the benefits of his wit. In doing so he can be thought to offer only amusement, and yet his is the wit of a special understanding which is well worthy of attention from the high. If the benefits Falstaff offers can be received and appreciated by the high only in the person of a truant prince, there is nevertheless profit in them for the high—and of course profit for the offerer, though it falls far short of his expectations. After Falstaff the low of the Shakespearean grotesque has a more thorough success in joining itself with the high, but the Falstaffian low must be given full credit for the success it has.

In bringing the Falstaffian low to this success Shakespeare takes the grotesque well beyond anything that seems to have been conceived for it in comment of his age. One may think of a remark upon the grotesque made by Montaigne. It is to be granted that Montaigne stands at some remove from developments in England that lead to the appearance of the Shakespearean grotesque on the stage. Nevertheless, it is curious that a man of Montaigne's late-Renaissance quality, writing over 400 years after St. Bernard of Clairvaux, should view the grotesque in a way much like the way we have found taken by St. Bernard. Montaigne too sees grotesque art only as monstrosity that has a strange and irrational appeal and has no relation to non-grotesque art. He calls his essays grotesque because, as he says by way of modesty, they are like fantastic painted figures shaped in casual fashion. They are to be thought of as deserving a place only outside the realm of right form. In the words of Florio's 1603 translation of *The Essayes*, Montaigne says at the beginning of his Chapter XXVII, 'Of Friendship':

Considering the proceeding of a Painters worke I have; a desire hath possessed me to imitate him: Hee maketh choise of the most convenient place and middle of every wall, there to place a picture, laboured with all his skill and sufficiencie; and all voyde places about-it, he filleth-up with antike Boscage or Crotesko works; which are fantastical pictures, having no grace, but in the varietie and strangenes of them. And what are these my compositions in truth, other then antique workes, and monstrous bodies, patched and huddled-up together of divers members, without any certaine or well ordered figure, having neither order, dependencie, or proportion, but casual and framed by chaunce?

> *Desinit in piscem mulier formosa supernè.*
> A woman faire for parts superior,
> Endes in a fish for parts inferior.

What is perhaps most surprising here is that Montaigne is not moved to say anything about a diverting play of imagination as having at least some part in the fashioning of 'monstrous bodies' in grotesque design as he knows it. He appears not to recognize as present something that by his account we should find there. Yet he is assuredly a man not without appreciation of the imagination in various forms. It seems hardly sufficient to say in explanation that he comments as he does simply because he reveres the classicism of Horace, whose line upon a representation of the mermaid quoted by him from the beginning of the *Ars Poetica* was written not that any play of fancy might be found in the imagined monstrous form it describes but merely that the form might be condemned for its lack of unity and simplicity.

Though low comedy in Elizabethan drama receives some contemporary English recognition for its diverting effect when it is interjected into decorous matter, there is in that recognition, as it now appears, a curiously limited range of view. The English genius that achieves Falstaff and the lesser figures of his kind seems, fortunately for posterity, to give itself the more fully to creating them in that it has only a rudimentary urge to deal with them in criticism. Very significantly, for example, it does not begin the debate which has discovered in Falstaff a part of his monstrous grotesqueness that makes him both a coward and not a coward. The longer this debate continues the more one is surprised that, as Arthur C. Sprague says at the beginning of a shrewd review of its arguments, 'for about a hundred and eighty years after Sir John Falstaff for the first time ran roaring from Gadshill, the fact of his cowardice was taken for granted'.[1]

---

[1] 'Gadshill Revisited', *Shakespeare Quarterly*, iv (1953), p. 125.

E

2

Falstaff is a 'monstrous body' in the tradition of grotesque animal and man-animal figures that Montaigne draws upon to characterize the form of his essays. At the same time he is part of something that may today be called, in Joycean terms, the 'fun-animal world', a world where man's animal 'comicity' can join with 'cosmicity'.[1]

What is done by imagery in the formation of Falstaff gives him monstrosity that ranges from the very simple to the very unsimple. At its simplest his monstrosity is made almost purely one of distortion. He is hugely fat, as we are not allowed to forget. Imagery that has to do merely with the fat Falstaff makes him almost completely simple in the narrow range of response it evokes for him. It may make him mildly unappealing, as he is, for example, in the guise of a 'woolsack', or a 'tun of man'. Or it may make him something thoroughly repellent, like a 'swol'n parcel of dropsies', a 'gross watery pumpion', or a 'stuff'd cloakbag of guts'.[2] What it does not make him is anything that truly takes hold of our sympathies.

In a way that often accords with his having a great burden of flesh Falstaff has within him an excessive amount of the animal. Imagery having to do with the animal Falstaff, sometimes in relation to the fat Falstaff and sometimes not, can make an additional presentation of unattractiveness.[3] Repulsively it shows him as animal material fit for the butcher's handling. He is a rolled-up ball of tallow, a 'whoreson obscene greasy tallow-catch', ready to be sent by the butcher to the candle-maker. He is more than that; he is a 'whoreson candle-mine', a candle-maker's reservoir of tallow. Or he simply answers to the name of Tallow. In another

---

[1] The terms are to be found with Joycean application in Jacques Mercanton, 'The Hours of James Joyce, Part II', trans. Lloyd C. Parks, *Kenyon Review*, xxv (1963), p. 96.

[2] My quotations from Shakespeare are as a rule from the text of G. L. Kittredge.

[3] For a view of animal metaphor in the presentation of Falstaff as adding to his comicality by disparaging him see Audrey Yoder, *Animal Imagery in Shakespeare's Character Portrayal*, New York, 1947, pp. 45 ff.

aspect he is a 'damn'd brawn', a fat pig ready for slaughter, and in still another (as Falstaff himself is made to suggest wryly in *The Merry Wives of Windsor*) he is no better than butcher's discard, a 'barrow of butcher's offal'. If his essentially beastly quality is to be given expression, he is a 'bolting hutch of beastliness', a receptacle for sifted and Simon-Pure beastly substance.

But the Falstaff of beastly substance is not entirely unable to get from the hands of the butcher into those of the cook and to be dressed as food. When he does, he can be not merely no longer repulsive but attractive in an extraordinary way. As food he can take on the special aura of attractiveness that is possessed by meat served on a festival occasion, and can even do so immediately after he has been found by the Prince to have the gross unattractiveness of a 'stuff'd cloakbag of guts'. The Prince in his next breath makes him into a 'roasted Manningtree ox with the pudding in his belly' (*1 Henry IV*, II. iv. 496). Since the 'pudding' here is a filling of meat, herbs, and other tasty edibles put into the animal's body cavity before roasting, there is reason enough to think of Shakespeare as allowing his imagination to leap from a picture of unattractiveness to one of attractiveness merely because belly-stuffing plays a part in each. But his arrival at the second picture through a 'chance' association with the first does not make the second less valid. Instead it gives it a special validity. The effect of the ox made savoury by stuffing is so much opposed to that of the cloakbag made unsavoury by stuffing that Shakespeare cannot have failed to recognize at once what he had done in making one of these images follow the other. He must have recognized and yet accepted. And his acceptance is proved to have been utterly right by what he does to Falstaff in general as he takes him well beyond the simplicities of being the fat man.

For Falstaff comes more and more to show that he has savouriness and unsavouriness strangely joined to help make him complexly monstrous. A savouriness to match that of the roasted Manningtree ox is found in Falstaff by Doll Tearsheet. She calls him a 'whoreson little tidy Bartholomew boar-pig' when he has just crossed swords with the obstreperous Pistol, driven him off, and returned to taking his ease at his inn with her and the Hostess (*2 Henry IV*, II. iv. 250–1). There is little to choose between roast pig as it was served traditionally at the fair held in Smithfield on St. Bartholomew's day and roast ox as it was served traditionally at the fair in Manningtree. Each is meat fit for a feast. But Doll is not made by Shakespeare to arrive in the same way as the Prince at a view of Falstaff as having so much as this to be said for him. She is made to come to it wholeheartedly and the Prince to come to it very much otherwise. Falstaff the Bartholomew boar-pig has just proved himself to his doxy as being, in her words, a 'whoreson little valiant villain', and is fully to her taste. Falstaff the Manningtree ox, however, has just been unmercifully made game of by the Prince for running away at Gadshill in a fashion that could only, by everyone in the tavern company except Falstaff, be taken as showing downright cowardice.

When a spectator of the two parts of *Henry IV* comes to Doll's commendation of Falstaff for defending her from the insults of Pistol, and doing so in no unknightly fashion, he may perhaps not agree with her that Falstaff is 'as valorous as Hector of Troy, worth five of Agamemnon'. Nevertheless, he may think that she has some reason to praise him. Falstaff carries off his bout with Pistol steadfastly and not without danger to his life. The encounter is not bloodless. We hear afterward that he has 'hurt' Pistol 'i' th' shoulder'. There has been shrewd thrusting by Pistol at Falstaff's precious belly, and this has been effectively parried. The spectator may at this point conclude that the balance has been tipped in favour of Falstaff's not being a coward. It may cross his mind that Falstaff at Gadshill can in truth have known the Prince all the while, just as he has said he knew him, and that there he ran away magnanimously instead of ignominiously, pretending fright in order to save the heir to the throne from endangering his life in the encounter. As for Falstaff's playing dead to save his life on the battlefield at Shrewsbury, one may easily come to think of this in retrospect as showing Falstaff's skill as a professional soldier in following the doctrine that all is fair in love and war.

But if the viewer of Falstaff's combat with Pistol does have thoughts like these, he is due to have them threatened and perhaps to find his judgement left completely at a stand. What happens next is Falstaff's picturing to Doll of the Prince as a shallow young-ster fit only to be a pantler and of Poins as a baboon, Falstaff all the while not knowing that these two stand behind him disguised as drawers. When the disguised two reveal themselves, Falstaff, pre-suming on what he has achieved in the way of place among the high, says to the Prince: 'I am a gentleman; thou art a drawer.' The Prince answers with a challenge that forces the avowed gentleman to engage or basely avoid: 'Very true, sir; and I come to draw you out by the ears.' Falstaff basely avoids. Sad to say, he fawns like any dog that crawls to his master intimating worthless-ness after being caught in dereliction. He answers the Prince: 'Thou whoreson mad compound of majesty, by this light flesh and corrupt blood, thou art welcome.' At this point Doll turns upon the knight who has fought and shed blood for her and dis-dains him utterly: 'How, you fat fool? I scorn you.' The viewer may well, for the moment at least, find himself entirely in agree-ment with her. He may see the suddenly abject Falstaff as a cowardly fat fool, even when he claims once more, as he has claimed at Gadshill, to have been protecting the Prince from harm. Falstaff's pretence this time, that he has only been saving the Prince from being admired by one of 'the wicked' who might seduce him, has nothing to be said for it except that it is amusingly pre-posterous. Since Gadshill the pretender has been falling off in cleverness, as he has been falling off in other ways that help to pre-pare for his final banishment.

It is partly as a dog currying favour in the domain of a higher order, sometimes shrewdly and engagingly, sometimes abjectly and revoltingly, that Falstaff must be seen when account is taken of the animality Shakespeare has given him. Marked preparation is made for the scene with Doll in which he becomes an offending dog that the Prince is ready to draw out 'by the ears' and punish. It comes in the scene where the Prince and Poins make their plan to wait upon him disguised as drawers and where the Prince, upon receiving a letter from him, offers the comment: 'I do allow this wen to be as familiar with me as my dog; and he holds his place, for look you how he writes' (*2 Henry IV*, II. ii. 115–17).

But when it is a matter of finding the dog in man, Falstaff can find in the Prince a wayward dog even before the Prince finds in him a too familiar dog. After the Lord Chief Justice has accused him of having misled the Prince, he is ready with the retort that the Prince is his dog and has misled *him*. The implication is that the Prince is held on a leash by Falstaff and has failed his master, who is dependent on him for guidance in the dark. This reversal of places between high and low is a triumphant achievement of presumption in the tradition of grotesque animality. Another achievement in the same tradition is that in which Falstaff, after being a bullcalf running and roaring for fear at Gadshill, imaged thus by the Prince, becomes a lion acting nobly there, imaged thus by himself. He becomes the king of beasts prevented by instinct from harming a true prince. Here there is admirable effrontery but of a lower grade. It merely joins Falstaff with the Prince in the ranks of human and animal royalty instead of pulling the Prince down from human royalty to animal subserviency and making Falstaff his human master.

3

Falstaff is complexly monstrous in the variety of his animality, but he is more intricately and at the same time more essentially monstrous in what he is as man and animal in one figure. The joining of the two in him has relationship to that figuration of doubleness in the mermaid which Montaigne takes to have an essentially grotesque quality, or to the figuration of doubleness in the centaur, equally favoured in the grotesque tradition of the Middle Ages and the Renaissance. But in Falstaff the beast and the non-beast are not joined with so violent an opposition to each other or so sharp a line of demarcation between them as to make a centaur form of the kind that Shakespeare brings the mad Lear to find in women:

> Down from the waist they are Centaurs,
> Though women all above.

But to the girdle do the gods inherit,
Beneath is all the fiend's (IV. vi. 126-9).

A figure of doubleness that may well be taken to exhibit an aspect of Falstaff is one put forward by his own wit but not for application to himself. He calls the Hostess an otter and, when the Prince succumbs to curiosity and demands his reason, says: 'Why, she's neither fish nor flesh; a man knows not where to have her' (*1 Henry IV*, III. iii. 144-5). The Hostess inevitably falls into the trap and protests that any man knows where to have her. Falstaff is a human being as much as the otter is a land creature and he is a brutish being as much as the otter is a water creature. The joining of man and beast in him, like the joining of creatures in the otter, is so much by way of interpenetration that it is not always easy to know where to have him. And of course he does not protest that he can be had.

For instance, Falstaff has all the animal desire that Lear attributes to centaur womanhood, but in him the beast is not by any means all beneath the girdle. It penetrates so far into what is above the girdle that it helps to make him the sensual man, the natural man *par excellence*, and yet it leaves generous space within him for a something more than natural. This other something affords him a lively understanding of his own grotesqueness as man and beast together, and of its relation to a general human grotesqueness with reaches of high and low even greater than his own. In *The Merry Wives of Windsor* he fails in many ways to come up to his best as revealed in earlier plays, but in a demonstration of that kind of understanding near the end of *The Merry Wives* there is no such failure. As he waits for the meeting with Mistress Ford and Mistress Page in Windsor Forest, disguised as Herne the Hunter with stag horns on his head, he offers a pagan prayer: 'Now, the hot-blooded gods assist me! Remember, Jove, thou wast a bull for thy Europa; love set on thy horns. O powerful love, that in some respects makes a beast a man; in some other, a man a beast! You were also, Jupiter, a swan for the love of Leda. O omnipotent love! how near the god drew to the complexion of a goose!' (v. v. 2-9). As he goes on to pray for 'a cool rut-time' and then welcomes Mistress Ford as 'My doe with the black scut', he is only another version of 'the town bull' among 'the parish heifers' which the Prince has made of him in relation to Doll Tearsheet and her kind. But he has just proved to have vision that is denied to stag or bull. The irony is that, though he is given vision to see love as making beast into man, the last thing anyone would expect him to be granted under any circumstances is a transforming love of which such vision could make him worthy. It seems to be commonly assumed that when the command was received from Queen Elizabeth to show Falstaff in love, if indeed there was that command, all Shakespeare could possibly show of Falstaff while keeping any artistic integrity was something like what he did show in *The Merry Wives*.

There is much truly that Shakespeare has not granted to Falstaff, but yet in what must be recognized as making him man there is that endowment of the very first order, his wit. He honours it duly and cherishes it as sacred. He looks up to it as Hamlet looks up to reason. For Hamlet it is reason that sets man most truly above the beast. For Falstaff it is wit, though he does not soliloquize philosophically on the subject. When Doll Tearsheet questions him about the association of the Prince with Poins, while these two are eavesdropping in disguise, she makes a suggestion: 'They say Poins has a good wit.' Falstaff replies by reducing Poins to presumptuous animal lowness: 'He a good wit? hang him, baboon!' (*2 Henry IV*, II. iv. 261). For Hamlet reason is that which looks before and after and reaches toward the understanding of all that has been or will be. For him wit is one of the ways of understanding provided by reason. For Falstaff wit is that which looks at all within the immediate foreground and reaches toward the understanding of a present situation. For him wit is reason itself. Because it is, he does not speak of the faculty of reason by name in any such way as Hamlet does. But Hamlet no less than Falstaff takes infinite delight in the play of wit.

Falstaff has been given a much more restricted human understanding than Hamlet's, but that which he has deserves his own high opinion of it, though this is saying much. It benefits by being

narrowly channelled. When Falstaff has the need to act, he is not
at all embarrassed by a wealth of conflicting perceptions such as
Hamlet's and he has no hampering doubt that he can prevail. His
faith is always in what he calls 'my admirable dexterity of wit' and
in the principle that 'a good wit will make use of anything'. By wit
which creates action as much as by that which creates idea and expression he comes to the achievement of authentic *tours de force*
and is masterful at bringing them about until Fortune first reduces
favour to him and finally becomes his foe.

Behind Falstaff is a line of notable Shakespearean clowns. To
say how much he rises above what they offer is to grant him all
that he claims about his wit as being both a virtue in himself and
a cause of that virtue in others. After him there are again notable
Shakespearean clowns, and they too do not come up to his level
of witty knowingness. But a Shakespearean grotesque figure that
after him at times rises even higher than he does is the fool, who
is related to the clown and occasionally gets the name of clown
but comes more and more to be distinguished from him.

In Falstaff, a participator in civil war as the companion of a
prince, clownage has travelled far beyond that of the rustic simpleton who can stumble amusingly across the stage of a conflict
among the great. It has left well behind what the early Shakespearean clown is in *Titus Andronicus*. A rustic in this play is per-
suaded by Titus to deliver a 'supplication' to the Emperor and,
because he is ignorant of the conflict between Titus and the Emperor, gets himself hanged (IV. iii and iv). From a world lying on
the margin of that in which there is a struggle for power he is
swept suddenly to the centre of the struggle and as suddenly swept
aside. He is granted a certain amount of grotesque genius in what
he says, though he is wholly without any proud Falstaffian understanding that he has it. The mad Titus thinks him a carrier of
letters from heaven concerning appeals made by Titus for justice
against the Emperor. Titus asks, 'What says Jupiter?' The clown's
answer, if one considers the fate that is all too soon to have
him hanged, seems to be given to him by an inspiring power
that mocks his innocent foolishness and makes him foreshadow

unwittingly his own downfall: 'Who? the gibbet-maker? He says
that he has taken them down again, for the man must not be
hanged until the next week.' The word-twisting that makes 'Jupiter' into 'gibbet-maker' is not to be thought of as produced by
wilful mistaking in the way that word-play often is with more
sophisticated Shakespearean clowns. When the name 'Jupiter' is
repeated to him, the clown is completely the honest simpleton as
he says: 'Alas, sir, I know not Jupiter. I never drank with him
in all my life.' Possibly, as has been suggested, there is an implication that he hears the name 'Jupiter' at first as 'gibbeter'.[1] If so, the
mocking power that inspires him provides a neater piece of word-
play than the bumbling clown can reproduce.

One never feels that Fate plays cat and mouse with Falstaff in
this way. In his knowingness he is simply not made to invite such
treatment. Fate does finally turn against him, but only after it
has many times befriended him and after he has often dared it
outrageously to prove that what Bardolph calls the 'monstrous
devices' of his wit are not equal to getting him out of any tight
place whatever.

Nor does one ever feel that Falstaff's wit shown in repartee is in
any way fortuitous. He is always the summoner and the master of
it. When the Lord Chief Justice lectures him, he is at his masterful
best in reply after reply. The Lord Chief Justice is not without
ability to turn a phrase himself when he says: 'There is not a white
hair on your face but should have his effect of gravity' (*2 Henry IV*,
I. ii. 182–3). But Falstaff has ability to transform neatly the
Justice's neatly turned phrase and thus with an imaginative eco-
nomy of words to present an aspect of his case. Each of those white
hairs, he answers, should have 'his effect of gravy, gravy, gravy'.
The Justice has happiness in taking the side of man the more-than-
animal, of man the stander on his dignity. But Falstaff has delight
in taking the side of man the food- and sex-desirous animal. He
takes that side with all the force of wit given to him as a man that
is actually a good bit more than animal. The implication is not
that he wants to be no more than an animal. It is that he wants to

[1] Helge Kökeritz, *Shakespeare's Pronunciation*, New Haven, 1953, p. 118.

be, and joyously is, an animal well endowed with man's mental cleverness, a witty animal, a monstrous animal.

Falstaff's play on the words 'gravity' and 'gravy' is thus different indeed from the play on 'Jupiter' and 'gibbet-maker' that in *Titus Andronicus* is given to the clown but is not made truly to belong to the clown. It is also very different from any ignorant or pretendedly ignorant word-play such as that in the typical malapropism.

Falstaff himself is always above committing malapropisms, but in the tavern world that he dominates they are, as one might expect, not lacking. It is strange that they come into that world late, for there is no reason why they should not come early, since they play a well developed part in the Shakespearean grotesque before the appearance of Falstaff. The Hostess is not at all a Mrs. Malaprop in *1 Henry IV*, but in *2 Henry IV* she becomes one of the best of the kind. It is plain that Shakespeare found the unknowingness of the Hostess to be something that demanded cultivation from him as it came on to prove itself.

The grotesqueness of the Hostess, being of a more primitive order than Falstaff's, has from the beginning an inevitable potentiality as a foil for Falstaff's. Her naïvety falls into the trap of his artfulness. When he tantalizingly calls her a 'thing', she presses him to say 'what thing, what thing', and he answers, 'Why, a thing to thank God on.' As his foil she is exactly the thing to be thankful for that he says she is, and of course she proves it by retorting, 'I am no thing to thank God on . . . and, setting thy knighthood aside, thou art a knave to call me so' (*1 Henry IV*, III. iii. 131–7). Falstaff's calling her an otter, which immediately follows this exchange, even draws the Prince into his trap of wit, in a manner that has just been spoken of. The truth is that both the Hostess and Falstaff are things to thank God on, though thanks are due more for Falstaff's existence than for hers.

Such lack of knowingness as is thus developed early in the Hostess invites naturally enough the later giving to her of a string of malapropisms. They begin at her first appearance in *2 Henry IV*, at the opening of the second act, when she has Falstaff arrested by the sheriff's officers Fang and Snare. There is much to be said for her making of 'homicidal' into 'honeysuckle' and 'homicide' into 'honeyseed' in the epithets 'honeysuckle villain' and 'honeyseed rogue' which she applies to Falstaff and Bardolph when they start the fray with the officers. In *The Merry Wives of Windsor* she has undergone great change in setting and some change in quality, just as Falstaff has. She is no longer Mistress of the Boar's Head in Eastcheap but servant to Doctor Caius. Yet she still has the name of Mistress Quickly, and still lends irony to it by being not so quick-witted as she would have to be to avoid malapropisms and keep from being made game of by Falstaff. Along with her name and her large lack of knowingness she brings over from *2 Henry IV* the pet exclamation 'what the good-yere!' (or 'what the goodier!'), apparently meaning about the same as 'what the devil!' As she produces her malapropisms in *The Merry Wives* Falstaff can find opportunity to benefit from her naïvety no less than he has bene-fited earlier. He does so notably when she defends Mistress Ford after he has been thrown into the Thames from the buck-basket. She makes the excuse that the servants of Mistress Ford misunder-stood what she directed them to do: 'She does so take on with her men! They mistook their erection.' It is for Falstaff to say, inevitably: 'So did I mine, to build upon a foolish woman's pro-mise' (III. v. 40–3).

4

With his wit Falstaff rises to eminence among Shakespeare's clowns and with his wit he also competes in higher company. It has been rightly said by M. M. Mahood that the word-play at which Shakespeare has made Falstaff so adept shows 'a vitality, a supercharged mental energy', of a kind that Shakespeare has given more generously only to Hamlet.[1] Discussion of what Hamlet's even more generous endowment of mental energy is made to con-tribute to the Shakespearean grotesque I leave to the ensuing chapter.

[1] M. M. Mahood, *Shakespeare's Wordplay*, London, 1957, p. 168.

It is plain that when Shakespeare gives word-play to clowns, he does so as a labour of love and not as a duty he thinks he owes to low comedy. And when he gives to many others of his human creations, some of them far from clownish, a mental energy disposed toward word-play, he manifestly does so because he has this mental energy in himself and takes pleasure in yielding to its urge, whether his dramatic purposes are comic or uncomic. The quarrel Samuel Johnson has with him on this score produces the famous reproach in the Preface to his edition of Shakespeare: 'A quibble was to Shakespeare the fatal Cleopatra for which he lost the world and was content to lose it.'

The concern with playing upon words that Shakespeare makes characteristic of clowns and fools he gives to them with true fittingness. By it they achieve grotesque figures of speech to reinforce whatever else helps to make them grotesque as figures of humanity. In its grotesqueness the pun is a monstrous union of incompatible things that has at times a complexity carried beyond doubleness. Its wholeness built of incompatibility is prone to be incompatible with and defiant of dignity. It fits Falstaff supremely well, sharp-witted as he is and monstrously constituted as he is, physically and otherwise. In its neatest, most closely joined, monstrous form he practises it with verve, as when he says, 'Indeed I am in the waist two yards about; but I am now about no waste: I am about thrift' (*The Merry Wives*, I. iii. 45–7). But he does not let himself be kept from practising at will the forms that are less neat, like his joining of the Lord Chief Justice's 'gravity' with 'gravy, gravy, gravy'.

It is with intensely moral scorn that Johnson condemns the joining of incompatible things in any pun at all. He calls word-play by the accusatory name of quibble, and seems to see its equivocation as no more worthy to be countenanced than the downright lie. He is blunt when he says that in gaining pleasure from use of the quibble Shakespeare 'was content to purchase it by the sacrifice of reason, propriety, and truth'. Strange as it may seem to us of the present day, Johnson reacts to the quibble as though it were a menace to man's reason and all else with which reason joins to build an ordered life in civilization. Certainly he sees it as something that eighteenth-century civilization, with its selective elegance, had removed justifiably from the literary scene, but to no such distance that it could not perhaps force its way back. After all, Addison in No. 61 of *The Spectator* (10 May 1711), showing himself to be as much though not so fervently against the quibble as Johnson, had given fair warning that 'it will again recover it self in some distant Period of Time, as Pedantry and Ignorance shall prevail upon Wit and Sense' (pedantry lending a hand, it seems, because pedants can be interested in the pun rhetorically and linguistically). We may infer that ours is that Period of Time which Addison foresaw.

Shakespeare's giving of the pun a part to play 'whatever be the dignity or profundity of his disquisition', to use Johnsonian terms for the extent of his quibbling, can now at times be looked at askance, though hardly looked down upon with true Johnsonian disapproval. But it can also be looked at with equanimity as producing what must be recognized as the characteristic Shakespearean 'uncomic pun'.[1] It can even be found to show that 'Shakespeare habitually thought in quibbles, if indeed "quibble" be the right term for what was one of the main roots of his poetic expression'.[2]

Realizing that the Shakespeare who expresses dignity and profundity thinks as characteristically in quibbles as the Shakespeare who expresses Falstaffian unregeneracy, one also realizes that when one of these Shakespeares echoes the other it is not always a matter of the second echoing the first in the way marginal medieval grotesques sometimes echo that to which they are attached. With Shakespeare the dignity which lack of dignity may echo is able in its own way to echo lack of dignity. It may do so in a way that shows itself as finding means to be profound in what lack of dignity may use to be grotesque.

In other words, the Shakespeare who creates Falstaff is not only

---

[1] Kenneth Muir, 'The Uncomic Pun', *Cambridge Journal*, iii (1950), pp. 472–85.

[2] *Hamlet*, ed. John Dover Wilson, New Cambridge Shakespeare, Cambridge, 1934, p. xxxv.

witty in himself but is the supporter of wit, or even the causer of wit, in the Shakespeare who creates figures that are non-grotesque. One may see something of the relationship in the passing on of two particular puns from Falstaffian to very different settings.

One of these puns is upon 'waist' and 'waste'. Falstaff, being what he is outwardly and inwardly, comes to the making of it as a matter of course. He makes the pun twice, once on an occasion in *The Merry Wives* which I have already mentioned, and before that in the following exchange between himself and the Lord Chief Justice in *2 Henry IV*:

Just. Well, the truth is, Sir John, you live in great infamy.

Fal. He that buckles himself in my belt cannot live in less.

Just. Your means are very slender, and your waste [Q *waste*, F 1 *wast*] is great.

Fal. I would it were otherwise. I would my means were greater and my waist [Q and F 1 *waste*, a common Elizabethan spelling] slenderer   (I. ii. 156–63).

A large waist for which buckling in by a belt is spoken of is not mentioned elsewhere in Shakespeare's plays except in *Troilus and Cressida*. There 'waist' is joined again with 'waste' in a pun.[1] The 'waste' is not the kind of which Falstaff is guilty, but nevertheless the reminiscence of Falstaff is strong. The dialogue in which the pun recurs is the debate carried on by the Trojans in poetic high style to decide whether Helen should be returned to the Greeks and the war over her should thus be brought to an end. When Hector argues on the ground of reason that Helen should be yielded up, Troilus is all for honour and scorns the thought:

> Fie, fie, my brother!
> Weigh you the worth and honour of a king
> So great as our dread father in a scale
> Of common ounces? Will you with counters sum

---

[1] For versions of the 'waist–waste' pun in Shakespeare see Helge Kökeritz, op. cit., p. 152. Kökeritz does not give the example from *Troilus and Cressida*, perhaps because he does not accept it. That it may be accepted seems to me clear, for reasons given.

The past-proportion of his infinite?
And buckle in a waist [Q and F 1 *waste*] most fathomless
With spans and inches so diminutive
As fears and reasons? (II. ii. 25–32.)

The waist that Falstaff's belt buckles in is a mighty expanse of flesh, acquired by self-indulgence and waste, and it is the outward and visible sign of his expansive substance of dishonour. The waist that Troilus is made to envision as an image of infinite worth and honour in his father the King—that is, in the Troy for which its king stands—is something that cannot be buckled in by any belt. It cannot because as a 'waist most fathomless' it is vast as infinity is vast. For an Elizabethan a 'waist' thus vast might aptly enough in a pun become a 'waste' because of the variant word forms 'waste' and 'vast', to which John Dover Wilson calls attention in a note on one of Horatio's lines in *Hamlet*:

In the dead waste [Q 2, F 1 *wast*, Q 1 *vast*] and middle of the night
(I. ii. 198).[1]

A 'vast' could be any immense space such as that covered by the ocean (as in 'this great vast', *Pericles*, III. i. 1), or could be an infinite space beyond the earth. So also a 'waste' could be either of these.[2] With warrant, then, one may interpret the quoted line of Horatio's as containing the 'waist–waste' pun, with the word 'middle' implying 'waist' and the word 'dead' implying 'waste' as connoting an expanse of desolateness.[3] Likewise with warrant one may interpret what Troilus says of Priam's and Troy's honour as containing the same pun, with the words 'buckle in' implying 'waist' and the words 'infinite' and 'fathomless' implying 'waste' as connoting an expanse such as outer space.

[1] *Hamlet*, edition cited, p. 153. Many editions have here 'the dead vast'. See C. T. Onions, *A Shakespeare Glossary*, 2nd edn., Oxford, 1925, under 'Waste' for the word as equivalent to 'vast', with a reference to this line from *Hamlet*.

[2] See 'Vast, *sb.*' and 'Waste, *sb.*' in the *Oxford English Dictionary*.

[3] But under 'Waist' in the *Oxford English Dictionary* the pun is seemingly not accepted, since this line in *Hamlet* is given as showing the word 'waist' (apparently uninvolved with 'waste' and 'vast') as being 'affectedly used' to reinforce the meaning of 'middle'.

The second of the two puns with which I am concerned as being reminiscent of Falstaff when they are given non-grotesque settings is also found in *Troilus and Cressida*, and comes only three lines after the occurrence there of the 'waist–waste' pun. Helenus scorns the arguments of Troilus that the 'waist–waste' of royal honour should not be buckled in by fears and reasons, and he begins his speech by saying,

> No marvel though you bite so sharp at reasons,
> You are so empty of them.

The 'reason–raisin' word-play thus used by Helenus was a homonymic pun in Elizabethan pronunciation. Falstaff resorts to it when he is hard pressed in cross-examination to give a reason for self-contradiction in his story of what happened at Gadshill.[1] Falstaff's version of the pun is: 'Give you a reason on compulsion? If reasons were as plentiful as blackberries, I would give no man a reason on compulsion, I' (*1 Henry IV*, II. iv. 263–6). Helenus adds depth in his version of the pun by the word-play in 'bite' and 'sharp' when he accuses Troilus of biting 'so sharp at reasons' because he is 'so empty of them'. He would have it that Troilus bites at 'reasons–raisins' in an animal's way of sharp attack, with the envious malice of a non-possessor, and at the same time bites at them in the way of sharp hunger, with the urging of an empty stomach. Shakespeare gives Helenus an achievement with the pun that goes much beyond Falstaff's.

Here, in what Troilus says and Helenus replies, Dr. Johnson presumably would find that Shakespeare contributes to his losing of a world—the world of the heroic Trojan tradition—by letting himself be seduced by a pair of quibbles that he has enjoyed before in low company and is now introducing into high company. But to do justice to Shakespeare one should realize, it would seem, that his poetic imagination is quite capable of making comic puns into uncomic upon occasion, or, to speak in Dr. Johnson's own

---

[1] Kökeritz, op. cit., pp. 138–9, gives other Shakespearean examples of the 'reason–raisin' pun besides Falstaff's, but does not give the one in *Troilus and Cressida*.

terms, of making seductive Cleopatras honest for the nonce. One
may say that it is the honesty of Shakespeare's poetic demand that
gives him such power in *Troilus and Cressida* when he lets his
imagination catch up for new use these puns that he has used
grotesquely in the creation of Falstaff. What draws his imagination
to do so is plain. In *Troilus and Cressida* the theme that brings the
puns into use is honour, as it is in the two parts of *Henry IV*, but
with a difference. That is to say, as between Falstaff and Troilus
the theme is honour dishonoured for one and honour honoured
for the other. Falstaff is an experienced older man with no desire
whatever for the honour of courage and faith-keeping, for himself
or anyone else, according to any usual concept of honour that is
held among warriors, lovers, or thieves; and he lives with outrageous satisfaction in the great infamy that this lack of virtue
brings him. As his opposite, Troilus is an inexperienced younger
man with an infinite desire for the honour of courage and faith-
keeping that he has conceived as warrior and as courtly lover, for
Troy and himself as participants in war and for Cressida and himself as lovers; and in love he fails to achieve his desire because of
Cressida's falseness, but in war achieves it for Troy and himself,
though with the sacrifice of both Troy and himself. Falstaff is presented comically as incapable of idealism in the least degree, and
Troilus is presented tragically as capable of idealism to the last
degree.[1]

One of the curiosities of Shakespeare interpretation is a denial
by Walter Whiter, the late-eighteenth-century critic, that there is
any pun offered intentionally by Shakespeare in the reply made
by Helenus to the passionate argument of Troilus that Trojan
honour must not be constrained by fears and reasons. Most certainly Whiter makes some remarkable observations on Shakespeare's subconscious associations shown in his imagery. He often
looks forward, across the nineteenth century, to our own explora-

----

[1] In an essay, 'Troilus in Shapes of Infinite Desire', *Shakespeare Quarterly*, xv
(1964), pp. 257–64, I have discussed the ironies involved in Shakespeare's giving
of contrasting forms of boundless idealism to Troilus the warrior and Troilus the
lover.

tions of the way one image, or more than one, may be summoned to Shakespeare's mind by the use he has just made of another. But Whiter very distinctly does not look forward to the twentieth century when he deals with Helenus' 'reason–raisin' pun. Then he is a good eighteenth-century man trying to save Shakespeare from 'false wit'. He tries to do so even at the cost of denying him sharpness of wit. The general direction of Whiter's concern with Shakespeare's imagination is indicated in the second part of the title of his book devoted to him, published in 1794: *A Specimen of a Commentary on Shakespeare Containing I. Notes on As You Like It. II. An Attempt to Explain and Illustrate Various Passages on a New Principle of Criticism Derived from Mr. Locke's Doctrine of the Association of Ideas.* What Whiter says about the pun given to Helenus is this: 'No quibble was intended by Shakespeare in the speech of Helenus. He himself was inadvertently entangled in this equivocal term *bite* by the similarity of the sounds *reasons* and *raisins*, and by the metaphor derived from *weighing* in a former speech' (p. 125). Whiter touches, however lightly, upon the essentials that here make the 'reason–raisin' pun what it is. He even points helpfully to the word 'weighing' in the preceding speech of Troilus, which has some claim to be noticed. But the entire word-play, with its central quibble and its supporting equivocal terms, he finds to be an accidental entanglement of ideas which has trapped the mind of Shakespeare—a great mind and therefore too rational to lend itself willingly to this sort of thing.

5

Shakespeare's favourite word-play is upon 'dear'.[1] The pun 'dear–deer' is of course part of it. Though Falstaff is not made to join in the use of that pun, he is made to provide occasion for its use, and to do so in a way that gives it a peculiarly strong effect as a part of his figuration. What the Prince says on the battlefield as he stands over the fallen but much alive Falstaff is moving, despite its judiciousness. It does not matter that the subject of the speech

---

[1] See M. M. Mahood, op. cit., p. 51.

is absurdly to rise again. The words said over him are as memorable
as they should be:

> Poor Jack, farewell!
> I could have better spared a better man.
> O, I should have a heavy miss of thee
> If I were much in love with vanity!
> Death hath not struck so fat a deer to-day,
> Though many dearer, in this bloody fray
>
> (*1 Henry IV*, v. iv. 103–8).

There is another farewell said to Falstaff in terms of the same pun.
This is to a Falstaff more sadly fallen—one who has fallen in spirit
and likewise in grotesque quality. After he has been put through
fiery purgation by sham fairies in Windsor Forest and has been
exposed as a dupe wearing deer's horns by those whom he would
have duped, including husbands he would have horned, Mistress
Ford takes leave of him thus: 'Sir John, we have had ill luck; we
could never meet. I will never take you for my love again, but I
will always count you my deer.' And Falstaff says, 'I do begin to
perceive that I am made an ass' (*The Merry Wives*, v. v. 120–5).
Completely dejected, putting himself down from the offered
animal level of deer to that of ass instead of rising from disaster
with the old ebullience of human wit, Falstaff reaches his nadir.

Thus each time the 'dear–deer' pun is used in a farewell to Falstaff it enforces what has been put forth of his monstrous doubleness as a man–animal. Opposed to and yet united with his
animality that can be 'deer' there is his humanity that can be
'dear'. The Prince's farewell has other word-play to adorn this
pun at its centre. The whole offering makes a handsome strew-
ment of wit over the supposed corpse of a witty 'fat deer'.

III

FALSTAFF AND THE CODES OF HIGH ENDEAVOUR

1

As the low is joined with the high in Falstaff himself, so his tavern world of low endeavour, where thieves and master-thieves are made, is joined with a political world of high endeavour where nobles and kings are made. The union is recurrently shown in the two parts of *Henry IV* to be one in which inner correspondences link the two worlds. But that the world of high endeavour is thus put before us in a satirical spirit as being really no different from the world of Falstaff and his fellows is not a conclusion that seems justified by Shakespeare's dramatization. This higher world seems to be no more made the butt of satire by being subtly joined to the Falstaffian world than the Falstaff of finished wit is made so by being joined to the Falstaff of gross animality through involved ties of common interest.

The typical 'better man', whom the reforming Prince has come to think 'dearer' than the 'fat deer' that he finds supposedly dead on the battlefield, is judged by the Prince's higher world to be of special worth in so far as he lives by a code of honour. Whatever antipathy this code may at times arouse today, Shakespeare clearly gives it a large measure of support, dramatically and poetically, as a valid expression of high endeavour. He does so despite errors of commission and omission that are to be charged against those whom he presents as trying to live by it.

Yet when Shakespeare provides a code of dishonour for Falstaff and makes him a devoted follower of it, his hand is again in large measure an accepting and supporting one. It is so generous with its support that the appeal of Falstaff to human sympathy becomes the demanding thing we know. Moreover, to use Joycean terms that I have referred to at the beginning of the foregoing chapter, the 'comicity' of Falstaff becomes undeniably a part of the 'cosmicity' of the drama of history.

2

What the Shakespearean grotesque sets itself to be on its way toward the achievement of Falstaff, as it opposes the high and yet joins with it ever more closely, may best be seen in three comedies where love rather than honour is the dominant theme of high endeavour. They are *The Two Gentlemen of Verona, Love's Labour's Lost*, and *A Midsummer Night's Dream*. Before considering the grotesque in *Henry IV* for its dramatic placement in relation to a code of honour I intend to consider the grotesque in these three comedies for a somewhat similar placement in relation to a code of love. I take each of the codes to be a Renaissance version of a cultural shaping of life evolved by the medieval warrior class as it grew ready to modify its unruliness. It has been well said, by more than one, that the code of courtly love is 'a feudalization of love'.[1] With it the warrior, who had learned in the service of his feudal lord the prime virtues of courage and troth-keeping that were given recognition by honour, could put these same virtues into the service of his lady. The ways are obvious by which courtly love could be extended, or even detached, from the milieu of warfare in which it had taken form and could become in a wider milieu what now has the name of romantic love.

In Launce and Speed of *The Two Gentlemen of Verona* the Shakespearean clown takes on pawky cleverness as a servant. He leaves behind him the knockabout physical comedy that the servant may be called upon to provide in *The Comedy of Errors* and *The Taming of the Shrew*, as he is beaten or has his ears wrung for misunderstanding. Both Launce and Speed possess wit that knows its way in action and in word manipulation. One may suspect the knowingness of Launce when, as a Mr. Malaprop, he speaks on his first appearance of having received his 'proportion, like the Prodigious Son', but it is not long before he makes it clear that he has ample

---

[1] By C. S. Lewis, for one, in *The Allegory of Love*, Oxford, 1936, p. 2.

capacity for wilful play with words. Moreover, both Launce and Speed show that clownishness has come to have a special significance in relation to that which it accompanies. It makes free with the high by making game of it, even directly and openly. Yet it is also able to echo the high in a way that is less an aping, either satiric or naïve, than it is a complementing of the high from below, or a showing of itself to be basic to the high at the same time that it is an opposite of it. It has been truly said that in considering 'the relation between the clown episodes and the leading themes, of love and friendship', in this play 'one has of course to bear in mind that in Elizabethan as in medieval work, burlesque need not mean belittlement of what is burlesqued'.[1]

Such complementing of the high while in opposition to it is found in the scene in which Launce discusses with Speed the qualities of the milkmaid—who is not too completely a maid—with whom he finally concludes that he is in love (III. i). The highest concern of the two gentlemen at the centre of the play's action is that of courtly love. Launce's master Proteus proves to have grievous faults of dishonesty when it comes to what is demanded of friend as well as lover by the codes of the courtly gentleman. Launce, who confesses that he is 'but a fool', nevertheless has the wit to know that his master 'is a kind of knave'. He himself, of course, is by implication a true knave, unburdened with any of the gentleman's obligations. But as a lover he can be honest—even devastatingly honest. He proceeds to demonstrate that fact as he considers the merits and demerits of his beloved. The list of her qualities which he has made out and which he asks Speed to read back to him is a primitive love poem dwelling meditatively upon the physical and spiritual constituents of a mistress but lacking any courtly compunction about recognizing that she has bad parts as well as good. In a sense it is a proto-sonnet written by the natural man to his love, but for himself, not for her. Shakespeare's Sonnet 130, 'My mistress' eyes are nothing like the sun', has to do

---

[1] Harold F. Brooks, 'Two Clowns in a Comedy (to say nothing of the Dog): Speed, Launce (and Crab) in *The Two Gentlemen of Verona*', *Essays and Studies*, xvi (1963), ed. S. Gorley Putt, p. 96.

with failings in a mistress and shows even less compunction but is written in a sophisticated spirit of paradox. It may be said that Launce is the natural man beginning to make distinctions and comparisons and that upon him the courtly lover must build in order to reach the unnatural refinement of belying his love 'with false compare' in the interest of an ideal of beauty. Beyond that refinement lies the even more unnatural refinement in Sonnet 130, which revolts against 'false compare' and makes the unlovely the beloved in the interest of an irrational truth.

As the natural man who is rightly enough the animal man, Launce quite fittingly can find praises for his mistress in animal terms: 'She hath more qualities than a water spaniel, which is much in a bare Christian. . . . "She can fetch and carry." Why, a horse can do no more. Nay, a horse cannot fetch, but only carry; therefore is she better than a jade' (III. i. 270–6). Other praises for her offer less poetic comparison, but the man who can lose his own identity in that of his dog Crab, a dog who, as he says, is only a cur, has found it in him to lift his beloved above a spaniel, with all the esteemed qualities of that breed. This, to echo him, is much in a bare Christian.

In the presentation of affinity between Launce and his dog Crab we meet with an extraordinary form of animal participation in the early Shakespearean grotesque. It produces monstrosity that accords with long-established grotesque tradition, but in a markedly new way. The dog who takes the part of Crab on the stage is called upon to do no acting except to sit solemnly by while his failure to come up to a moral standard is talked about as though he were a human being. His mere sitting and solemn listening have the effect of making him a presumptuous dog. By these actions he shows acceptance of what Launce by his reproaches is holding him up to be, a dog that has taken on moral perceptions and obligations. Here there is a subtle kind of aping to make one think of the animals that ape man more openly in medieval manuscript illuminations. In Launce's reproaches, however, we learn that poor Crab has fallen into great trouble because it has been beyond his capacity to emulate 'gentlemen-like dogs' under the ducal table among whom he has thrust himself. An indiscretion of his, an answer to a call of nature which the sophisticated dog that is raised above the level of the natural dog does not yield to in such surroundings, has almost got him whipped and hanged. Launce has saved him by being whipped in his stead. What Launce has done to take the punishment on himself has been to say in all simplicity ' 'twas I' after Crab has been accused of the indiscretion.

The bond between Launce and Crab which brings that ' 'twas I' from Launce is strong enough to produce rank confusion in Launce as to which is the dog and which himself. This is to be seen in his version of what happened at his parting from his family in Verona to follow his master to Milan. There was much weeping. Even the cat (strangely better at assuming humanity than the dog that's friend to man) took to 'wringing her hands', while cruel-hearted Crab shed not one tear. As Launce acts all this out with properties at hand, including the dog, he comes to lose himself in the dog and the dog in himself: 'Now, sir, this staff is my sister . . . This hat is Nan, our maid. I am the dog. No, the dog is himself, and I am the dog. O, the dog is me, and I am myself. Ay, so so!' (II. iii. 20–5.)

The doubleness of Launce as man–animal is in the end made grotesque to the point of complete paradox by his seeing of himself as wholly dog at the same time that he sees himself as wholly man. His wit is by no means of the best but is good enough to make him monstrous in a somewhat Falstaffian way by its incompatibility with the excessively animal part of him to which it is firmly joined.

In *The Two Gentlemen of Verona* the low seems to acquire the impulse of love at the prompting of the high as servant echoes master, but in *Love's Labour's Lost* things are for a time turned the other way round. At the beginning of that play the high seems prompted by the low. Throughout the action the low provides in its practice of love what may be called elemental support for the high, even after it turns from leading the high in love to following it.

When the King of Navarre and his lords enter upon their

pseudo-monastic three-years' regimen, according to which, as late Renaissance rather than medieval ascetics, they have sworn

> To fast, to study, and to see no woman
>
> (IV. iii. 292),

they enjoin their grotesque attendants to quell what Costard calls 'the simplicity of man to hearken after the flesh'. It is Costard, the clown of complete simplicity, who heads the procession of those who break the rule against love. Next comes Armado, who, as a braggart soldier and a fantastic though by no means witless user of words, is one of the low but is higher in the scale than Costard. His downfall is brought about by Jaquenetta, the same country wench with whom Costard has just been apprehended. With no loss of time defection begins among the high, and Berowne, the outstanding wit among the lords, follows Armado. After him the procession gathers one courtly lover after another.

Berowne can muse upon Rosaline, his conqueror among the attendant ladies of the Princess of France, in the spirit of Shakespeare's Sonnet 130:

> A whitely wanton, with a velvet brow,
> With two pitch-balls stuck in her face for eyes
>
> (III. i. 198–9).

Upon yielding to her he finds her eyes indeed 'nothing like the sun'. But yet he is brought 'to sigh for her! to watch for her! / To pray for her!' For the King and all his lords the low in the form of the natural man invades the precincts of the high and insists upon presence there. But it does not capture the high. It invades the poetry of Berowne's musing and makes eyes into pitch-balls. Nevertheless an aspiration of courtly love creates a religion of love in his poetry later and gives eyes an authority of holy writ:

> From women's eyes this doctrine I derive:
> They are the ground, the books, the academes,
> From whence doth spring the true Promethean fire
>
> (IV. iii. 302–4).

The low in *Love's Labour's Lost* not only fails to capture the high but suffers finally from what anyone with sympathy for the lowly can only take to be heartless cruelty in the high. From the beginning the high has planned to enjoy in the midst of its elevated concerns a contribution of 'quick recreation' from the low. In the end, when the ambitious Show of the Worthies is offered by the low as part of such recreation, the courtly audience engages in extended baiting of the poor actors, whose 'zeal strives to content' but whose achievement can only be as grotesque as they are themselves. Holofernes the pedant assumes the part of Judas Maccabaeus and is baited off the stage before he has well begun to act it. One can but find justice in his parting words: 'This is not generous, not gentle, not humble' (v. ii. 632–3). When the affairs of the high in the drama are brought to their conclusion in an access of seriousness, the whole group of grotesque actors are waved aside by Berowne with the line:

> Worthies, away! The scene begins to cloud
>
> (v. ii. 730).

Of subtler form but of quality related to what we find here are the baiting and tricking of Falstaff by the Hal who is a madcap prince and the putting of Falstaff the entertainer to one side by the Hal who has become a serious king.

Love's Labour's Lost is linked to *A Midsummer Night's Dream* in that both plays come to an end with an offering of grotesque entertainment staged by the low for the high at which the high does this kind of baiting as the low is engaged upon its earnest acting. After a different fashion *A Midsummer Night's Dream* is in turn linked to *Romeo and Juliet* in that its Pyramus and Thisby interlude matches grotesquely the tragedy of young love in the other play. It seems that Shakespeare wrote these three plays in the two-year period 1594–6. *Love's Labour's Lost* is usually taken to be the earliest. Which is the earlier of the other two is a vexing question. What makes the question interesting in connection with the development of the early Shakespearean grotesque is the possibility that the Pyramus and Thisby interlude is not a 'burlesque' or 'parody' of *Romeo and Juliet*, written after that tragedy by a

Shakespeare seeking relief 'like a horse kicking up its heels when let into pasture'.[1] Aside from its being a 'most lamentable comedy' of love fit for the amusement of young lovers in *A Midsummer Night's Dream* who have passed beyond having anything to lament, it may be a grotesque excursion attractive to Shakespeare for its own sake, upon which he discovered, perhaps to his surprise, that he was moved to turn from the writing of a succession of love comedies to the writing of a love tragedy. After all, Arthur Brooke's poem on the tragical love of Romeus and Juliet, with a story challengingly close to that of Pyramus and Thisby, was at hand. If it is thus that *Romeo and Juliet* came to be written, then it provides another example than the one in *Love's Labour's Lost* of the high romantic that is shown the way in love by the grotesque low.

It is noteworthy that in *A Midsummer Night's Dream* Theseus is made to speak in defence of the actors of the Pyramus and Thisby interlude in a vein of eloquent nobility, and that when he presides over its presentation the baiting of actors is moderated and never goes so far as to hound anyone from the stage. In this fact is one measure of a depth in the play never reached in *Love's Labour's Lost*. In that play the Princess of France, urging the resisting King of Navarre to allow the actors to present their performance in spite of his scorn for their ability, has only this to say of what the grotesque low can give to the high:

> That sport best pleases that doth least know how:
> Where zeal strives to content, and the contents

[1] Geoffrey Bullough, ed., *Narrative and Dramatic Sources of Shakespeare*, i, 2nd edn., 1961, p. 376. G. L. Kittredge, ed., *The Complete Works of Shakespeare*, New York, 1936, p. 1005, thinks that *A Midsummer Night's Dream* is probably the earlier play and scorns the idea that *Romeo and Juliet* is parodied in it. A conclusion that arguments for *A Midsummer Night's Dream* as the earlier play are at least as good as those against is reached by Madeleine Doran, 'Pyramus and Thisby Once More', *Essays on Shakespeare and Elizabethan Drama in Honor of Hardin Craig*, Columbia, Missouri, 1962, p. 161. Support for the view that *Romeo and Juliet* is the earlier and is parodied in the other play is offered by Kenneth Muir, *Shakespeare's Sources*, i, London, 1957, p. 46. E. K. Chambers, to whose dating of Shakespeare's plays I have given consideration throughout these chapters, makes *Romeo and Juliet* 'preferably' the earlier, *William Shakespeare: A Study of Facts and Problems*, Oxford, 1930, i. 345.

Dies in the zeal of that which it presents.
Their form confounded makes most form in mirth
When great things labouring perish in their birth

(v. ii. 517–21).

But Theseus, speaking to the resisting Hippolyta, who pities the actors and does not wish to see in them 'wretchedness o'ercharg'd / And duty in his service perishing', has this to say:

> Our sport shall be to take what they mistake;
> And what poor duty cannot do, noble respect
> Takes it in might, not merit.
> .   .   .   .   *
> And in the modesty of fearful duty
> I read as much as from the rattling tongue
> Of saucy and audacious eloquence.
> Love, therefore, and tongue-tied simplicity
> In least speak most, to my capacity
>
> (v. i. 90–105).

The Princess of France does not feel the compulsion of *noblesse oblige*. Theseus does. She wants merely to laugh at and look down upon clownish incompetence. He wants to laugh at it but accept it, make allowance for it, and even show a certain respect for its tongue-tied simplicity. In key with all that Theseus thus expresses, *A Midsummer Night's Dream*, when it brings Bottom and his fellow mechanicals upon the scene, contrives to give the grotesque low a due place among the orders of life and a quality that draws fellow feeling from life other than its own, however much it also draws laughter. The advance made beyond *Love's Labour's Lost* in this respect is plain. There is reason enough for the appeal Bottom and his company have had for a wider audience than that of Theseus' court.

Bottom, when all has been said in his favour, remains still very much the naïve clown, though he has an extraordinary power to convince his companions that he is a man of parts and to convince us that he is well worth our attention. He is the first among

Shakespeare's grotesque figures with a winning nature at all comparable to Falstaff's. But a fully knowing wit, a sophisticated art, and an ability to entertain highness while hobnobbing with it, instead of merely entertaining it across a social barrier, must be added to make a Falstaff.

With much justice Bottom can be called an ass. He is called so in the ordinary way of denigration by those among the high. But it is to be recognized that he is generously and attractively endowed as a monstrous man–animal. He yearns to play the lion's part, not merely because he longs to rise above asininity and be nobly leonine but also because, just as he aspires to be man in various forms (even to lisp like a Thisby), he likewise aspires to be variously animal (even to roar like any sucking dove instead of like a true lion). It is a nice touch in the Pyramus and Thisby interlude that makes Pyramus, and through him makes Bottom as actor of his part, a 'most brisky juvenal' and at the same time a horse with fine points. He is

> As true as truest horse, that yet would never tire
>
> (III. i. 98).

The joining of humanity with animality in the interlude allows the lion to speak. There is the baiting comment from the audience that 'one lion may, when many asses do' (v. i. 155).

Bottom is a hero among his fellows simply because he sees and does things with a superior naïvety of naturalness that comes from animality. For his naïvety to work as admirably as it does, it must have greater freedom from sophistication than the naïvety of his fellows. Because of its quality Puck calls him

> The shallowest thickskin of that barren sort
>
> (III. ii. 13).

It makes him, of course, the one in his group who is the most susceptible to magical 'translation' into a man with an ass's head.

When Oberon hears that the sleeping Titania, under the spell he has put upon her, has waked and now 'with a monster is in

love', he thinks the result better than he could have devised. He
has told Puck that after he has anointed Titania's eyes

> The next thing then she, waking, looks upon
> (Be it on lion, bear, or wolf, or bull,
> On meddling monkey, or on busy ape)
> She shall pursue it with the soul of love
>   (II. i. 179–82).

In the incantation used at the anointing of her eyes he has likewise
given the possible object of her infatuation only as some beast.
Maliciously he is more than happy to accept Bottom as her beloved. A beast is low in Nature's order, but a monster he takes to
be lower still in that it is an aberration of Nature.

Bottom experiences grotesquely the adventure in which a hero
taken as lover by a lady of the faerie is conveyed to an enchanted
world from which he can escape only after suffering an impair-
ment of his sense of mortal reality. As he enters that world Bottom
is blissfully unconscious that he is yielding to the enticements
of a Titania playing Morgan the Fay. And he is most pitifully
unaware that he is to have the experience of a more than ordi-
narily privileged lover in a romance. After the experience all he
can remember is a dream that 'hath no bottom'.

The love interlude of Pyramus and Thisby and the love tragedy
of *Romeo and Juliet* show an extraordinary extension of the joining
of grotesque and non-grotesque beyond the bounds of a single
play. But the love of Romeo and Juliet is joined within its own
dramatic setting to a grotesqueness that is, in the main, of quite
another kind than any in *A Midsummer Night's Dream* or related
early comedies. What is found in this union of opposites looks
forward beyond the Falstaff plays. I leave it to be discussed in connection with the later Shakespearean grotesque.

3

Where the theme is love, we have found in one comedy a princess of France superciliously accepting the low as providing the
kind of sport for the high which 'best pleases' because it 'doth
least know how' and as providing the sport in a 'form confounded'

which 'makes most form in mirth'. But in that play the low
actually does more for the high than the princess thinks. It leads
in a dance of love in which both high and low engage. In another
comedy, probably the next written, we have found a duke of
Athens accepting with 'noble respect' a 'tongue-tied simplicity',
which, though it does not show the way of love to those of the
high that are presented in the play, may perhaps deserve credit for
bringing a love tragedy into being in a following play.

Where the theme is honour, we find in the two parts of *Henry IV*
and in *Henry V* a prince of England accepting adventurous experience of the ways of dishonour as a strange but effective under-
pinning for a kingship that can say on the battlefield:

> But if it be a sin to covet honour,
> I am the most offending soul alive
> (*Henry V*, iv. iii. 28-9).

The Falstaff who is the King of Misrule and from whom the Prince
turns away to be King of England is no figure of tongue-tied
simplicity that can be comfortably scorned by the high. Further-
more, he is far indeed from showing the 'modesty of fearful
duty' that a Duke Theseus can think deserving of noble respect.
He goes beyond his Shakespearean predecessors in depth of grotesqueness by articulately expressing opposition to a code of the
high and at the same time contributing more than they do of
elemental support to the high.

As Falstaff takes on form that is in contrast to form approved by
the high and yet echoes it, there is small temptation to think of
him as the natural man satirized. However much he may be made
to show failings in comparison with his betters, he has that about
him which keeps one from seeing him as held up by Shakespeare
to ridicule. Indeed his betters sometimes suffer by comparison
more than he does. They can come down embarrassingly from
heights of code-directed action to which he does not aspire and
from which he thus cannot fall. Nevertheless they too resist being
regarded as subjects of ridicule. In the two parts of *Henry IV* the
grotesque has developed to a point where it can have a dramatic

weight to balance that of the non-grotesque to which it is attached and can share with the non-grotesque in demanding complex response from the viewer.

At the beginning of *1 Henry IV* a man who has come to the honour of kingship reveals that as he has risen he has also fallen. Gaining highest honour in the arena of the world he has lost integrity within himself. He stands accused by a double conscience, by his sense of right according to his code of honour and by his sense of right according to the code of Christianity. These codes come together in condemnation of the act of thievery compounded with murder that he has committed to obtain the crown, the code of honour condemning it because the former possessor was his liege lord, and the code of Christianity because that possessor was a fellow man as well as an anointed king. The crusade Henry says he is undertaking as the play opens is to be an expiation offered to both honour and Christianity. Henry, who has proved to be so disloyal a warrior under Richard II as to supplant him, is now to prove himself loyal in arms to one deserving of allegiance who is to be counted greater than Richard:

> As far as to the sepulchre of Christ—
> Whose soldier now, under whose blessed cross
> We are impressed and engag'd to fight—
> Forthwith a power of English shall we levy
>
> (I. i. 19–22).

The expiation is never to become reality and that which is to make it impossible begins to show itself even as he finishes his opening speech. Henry faces the necessity of fighting at home to keep his stolen crown from being stolen from himself, burdened though he must be with the sense that a curse has been laid upon it. His never-appeased conscience finally leads him to say on his death-bed to his heir:

> God knows, my son,
> By what by-paths and indirect crook'd ways
> I met this crown
>
> (*2 Henry IV*, IV. v. 184–6).

The theme of conscience thus appearing at the outset and running through the drama is part of the tradition of the English morality play that helps to give *Henry IV* its form. Also, the theme of thievery is related to much in that tradition that shows the depths to which fallen man can come. But Shakespeare is giving a twist in more ways than one to what he draws from the tradition. Henry IV has fallen but he cannot achieve the remission of sin that Humanum Genus often achieves by repentance when mercy is shown to him in the traditional morality. The fall in this case only begins with Henry and must be extended onward from him into the following generation and downward from the world of the court and courtiers to that of the tavern and tavern-haunters. The son who is to inherit the kingdom must explore thievery in low quarters and rise from that depth before the curse can be removed from the crown that was gained by thievery in high quarters.

The Prince is not shown as being tempted and falling. When we first see him, he has already descended as far as he is to go, and we quickly gather that it is by a fate for which his father is responsible that he has come to be where he is. He seems to have been so constituted by this fate that he has inevitably sought out the tavern world and as a wilful scapegrace indulging in thievery has become a painful reminder to his father of the wrong-doing that obtained the crown. It is soon driven home that the Prince is not an innocent and unperceiving Mankind who is being trapped into doing evil by a clever Vice. That Shakespeare draws avowedly on the tradition of the morality play in shaping Falstaff and making him under one aspect, given him by the Prince, a 'grey Iniquity', a 'reverend Vice', and an 'abominable misleader of youth', is plain.[1] But one of the twists here given to the morality tradition is the making of the Vice into the biter bit. No matter how clever Falstaff is, he is not to be found tricking the Prince. Where one

---

[1] Good brief conspectuses of what can be said on this matter are offered by R. W. Babcock, 'Mr. Dover Wilson, the Critics, and Falstaff', *Shakespeare Association Bulletin*, xix (1944), p. 120, and A. R. Humphreys, ed., *1 Henry IV*, Arden Shakespeare, London, 1960, pp. xli ff.

of these two tricks the other, it is always the Prince who does the tricking and he does it with less mercy than whole-hearted affection should show. Moreover, Falstaff as a Vice who is a biter bit becomes a misleader misled and by his own account has thus been made 'little better than one of the wicked' and put sadly in need of reform: 'Thou hast done much harm upon me, Hal—God forgive thee for it! . . . I'll be damn'd for never a king's son in Christendom' (*1 Henry IV*, i. ii. 102–9).

It must be granted that there is indeed a harm done upon Falstaff by the Prince, though not the corruption of an innocent man who 'knew nothing', as Falstaff claims. The harm done makes for a strange subjection for a Vice to have to his Mankind. The Prince is fascinated with observing the ways of genius by which Falstaff goes counter to the life of virtue and honour, and he is thus caught indeed by Falstaff the Vice, but Falstaff in turn is fascinated with the fascination his genius exercises upon royalty and is thus caught by the Prince. The Prince eggs him on to the enlargement of his scope. Falstaff responds and at times shows a rather pitiful side as a performing pet. The Prince can even play the part of a Mankind tempting his Vice, as when he meets Falstaff's vow of reform with the question 'Where shall we take a purse tomorrow, Jack?'

But as Mankind the Prince has a conscience. His is by no means a conscience like his father's, and here again there is a twist given to what comes from the morality tradition. The conscience of the father, as it takes form at the end of *Richard II*, is a conventional one that draws from him the expression of a need

> To wash this blood off from my guilty hand

and the expression of a sorrow

> That blood should sprinkle me to make me grow.

The conscience of the son gets expression as early as the second scene in *1 Henry IV*. It looks forward with approval to a temporary continuation of 'idleness' and 'loose behaviour' on the part of its possessor, though not, be it noted, to anything more heinous than that. Approval of a departure from rectitude so mild and

transitory it considers justifiable if the offender, by giving his word
of honour even in the midst of dishonour, can make this promise:

> I'll so offend to make offence a skill,
> Redeeming time when men think least I will.

In what is thus pledged no looking back in sorrow or repentance
is involved. It appears that 'redeeming time' does not mean 'making amends for wasted time', as this phrase has often been taken
to mean. Time in the future is to be redeemed, or made the most
of, by the Prince according to recognized codes for good employ-
ment of it, but without redemption being thought of as atoning
for what has been done with time in the past. That the phrase has
such reference to immediate time only is plain from several
examples of Elizabethan usage as well as from the relevant Biblical
use in Ephesians 5: 16, 'Redeeming the time, because the days are
evil'.[1] When Richard Wever's pre-Elizabethan morality *Lusty
Juventus* shows Good Counsell instructing Juventus before he has
been brought by the tempting forces of evil to engage in time-
wasting sin, the instruction includes an interpretation of that
Biblical text:

> Sainct Paul vnto ye Ephesians geveth good exhortacion
> Saying, walke circūspectly, redeming the time,
> That is to spend it well, and not to wickednes enclyne.[2]

The Prince never does confess himself guilty of anything so
flagrant as 'wickedness', and this fact turns out to have a many-
sided significance. For one thing, Shakespeare is looking toward
what he is to do with the young King in *Henry V* and is making
the Prince much less irresponsible than he is in *The Famous Victories
of Henry the Fifth*. He is giving him less culpability, as is evident,
for example, in his having him make restitution of Gadshill loot.
For another thing, Shakespeare is concerned with a distinction
between a code of honour and the code of Christianity as these

---

[1] On this subject I find convincing what is said by Paul A. Jorgensen, ' "Redeeming Time" in Shakespeare's *Henry IV*', *Tennessee Studies in Literature*, v
(1960), pp. 101–9.
[2] Edition of John S. Farmer, Tudor Facsimile Texts, London, 1907, sig. Aiii^r.

apply to wrong-doing, a distinction that remains clear, no matter how far the code of honour may draw support from the Christian code or lend support to it.[1] From the beginning he gives the Prince a sense of need to forswear dishonour but not to forswear any part of dishonour as having the guise of sin. The Prince is always incapable of desiring, as his father desires, to atone for sin by leading a crusade. When he becomes King, he leads an army against French holders of land claimed for England instead of against pagan holders of land claimed for Christendom. He is concerned to have ecclesiastical sanction for this venture, but he engages in it to redress English honour. There is a great difference between father and son as they are affected by codes. The father is of an old order of men and the son is of a new.

The most important thing of all to be considered for present purposes is that Shakespeare makes the Prince a means of showing how the grotesque can be banishable at the call of reformation and yet prove to have a place of serviceability in the scheme of things that renders it ultimately unrejectable. At the beginning of *1 Henry IV* there is an all too simple finding within the grotesque of serviceability to the non-grotesque. It is made by the Prince when he promises an eventual redeeming of time. He looks to his close association with the grotesque to provide in its 'unyok'd humour' of idleness a succession of 'playing holidays' that will make him all the more wanted by the world before he pleases 'again to be himself'. He also looks to it, even less engagingly, to provide him with a bad reputation that will give him a gratifying opportunity to startle all England with his reformation. Here the Prince is a politician as practical as his father was when he achieved popularity before capturing the throne. And here the Prince in his single-mindedness offers a justification of the grotesque that has been offered by many. It is that the grotesque low is desirable just

---

[1] As is well argued by Paul N. Siegel, 'Shakespeare and the Neo-Chivalric Cult of Honor', *The Centennial Review*, viii (1964), pp. 39–70. The love of honour shown by Shakespeare as love of a virtue for itself and also as love of fame for practice of that virtue is commented upon by Curtis Brown Watson, *Shakespeare and the Renaissance Concept of Honor*, Princeton, 1960, pp. 206 ff.

as a contrast to the non-grotesque high. It glorifies the high by being a foil to it but at the same time offers a 'relief' from it that is much appreciated by mere humanity, which is inclined to tire of any contemplation or pursuit of high seriousness and high endeavour. But we see the Prince becoming indebted to the grotesque for much more than he thus envisions. For it grows clear that the grotesque is not to be set apart from the non-grotesque as he thus sets it apart. Joined with the non-grotesque it contributes to it and helps to make it what it is. It has that in it which must be passed on to and reshaped by the non-grotesque and which must retain a part of its original quality, no matter what reshaping of it is done. A prince of England who learns at first hand how much the grotesque can give to the non-grotesque may gain the particular kind of knowingness that will make him a Henry V.

Among the many various correspondences bonding the grotesque to the non-grotesque in *Henry IV* and *Henry V* those that have to do with thievery are dominant.[1] Like the others these can often be considered as echoes. At the beginning of the action the robbing of robbers at Gadshill can be seen as low thievery that echoes in grinning mockery the high thievery in the course of which the man who is to become Henry IV has his inheritance stolen by Richard II and then himself steals Richard's crown. But it is quickly apparent that echoing between high action and low can be turned about so that, instead of low echoing high, there is high echoing low and the effect is that of irony inadvertently provided by the high. The scene in which Hotspur, Worcester, and others plot to rob Henry of his kingdom echoes in that way the scene at the tavern in which the robbery at Gadshill is plotted, and it is all the more effective in that it is the scene immediately following. Still another, and more inclusive, kind of echoing comes climactically in *1 Henry IV*. When the Prince triumphs by killing Hotspur, high action reflects previous variations in both high action and low on the theme of the robber robbed and draws them together in a final closeness. In this victory the Prince robs

---

[1] This theme of thievery is perceptively dealt with by Robert Hapgood, 'Falstaff's Vocation', *Shakespeare Quarterly*, xvi (1965), pp. 91–8.

Hotspur of honours gained in battle as a noble predator and puts them in place of his own dishonours gained partly on the highway as an ignoble predator. And when the robber Falstaff, after administering a second death to the victim, is allowed to take from the robber Prince a part of these honours taken from the robber Hotspur, there is an amiable joining of high and low to extend this echoing.

In the trilogy of *Henry IV* and *Henry V* one senses a sharing of substance by grotesque and non-grotesque that has much human history behind it. It appears that honour itself could not be what it is without what it shares with the grotesque. In the background is the natural man as he has been before creating a code of honour capable of taking over his combativeness and predatoriness to put form upon them. As a being merely grotesque he can be seen in medieval manuscript illuminations, struggling nakedly and barehandedly with all that surrounds him, including his fellows. Then when he comes to have armour upon his body, weapons in his hands, and a horse to ride, he is a man of prey that can be seen in one form as grotesque and in another as non-grotesque. In words used by Henry IV blood must sprinkle him to make him grow. As a man of prey he cherishes a hawk upon his fist as a bird of prey and thinks of it as having worthiness like his own to be called noble because of its fierceness of heart. But by now he has in his non-grotesque form treated his animal combativeness and predatoriness in a way no animal could have treated it and has made it worshipful. He has embodied it in a faith and, with human idealism added to animal instinct, he vows in accord with his faith to fight to the death if challenged as an individual or if challenged along with others to whom he has committed himself as a fellow combatant. He has become a man who preserves the honour of courage for himself and keeps his word of honour as given to others—if he can succeed in living up to the ideal he has created. Without the basic animality that he carries with him he could not be what he has become, for his honour could not have vitality as honour. He can look down upon the grotesque natural man standing beside him who refuses to grasp at honour, but the natural man dwelling within him is nevertheless a grotesque support for all he has of the non-grotesque.

The man of honour at a later stage may of course take the practice of his faith into a field quite other than that of physical combat. But in what Shakespeare has dramatized from the reigns of Henry IV and Henry V the man of honour is still very much on the battlefield. He is found there in many forms and in many gradations of faithfulness.

4

Falstaff is not the complete image of anti-honour that he makes himself out to be in the well-known soliloquy where he says of honour, 'I'll none of it' (*1 Henry IV*, v. i. 128–39). He confirms his monstrosity of doubleness by the way he supports honour as well as rejects it.

Valour is represented as the first demand made upon men by honour, and Falstaff can be found demanding valour with all the very considerable eloquence Shakespeare has given him. He does so in his soliloquy on the virtue of sherris-sack (*2 Henry IV*, iv. iii. 92–135). Here we have a prose paean not merely to sack but also to the men that sack can bring into being. These are not 'demure' and 'sober-blooded' boys who beget wenches when they marry and who 'are generally fools and cowards'. They are in every way men, outstanding in both their sophisticated and their natural faculties. They allow sack to fill their brains with 'nimble, fiery, and delectable shapes' which their tongues can make into 'excellent wit'. More heroically, they allow sack to make their bodies into puissant small kingdoms that rouse themselves valiantly for warfare. Sack works thus on a man: 'It illumineth the face, which, as a beacon, gives warning to all the rest of this little kingdom, man, to arm; and then the vital commoners and inland petty spirits muster me all to their captain, the heart; who, great and puff'd up with this retinue, doth any deed of courage.'

No follower of the religion of honour could object to the poetic ardour that Falstaff brings to this praise of courage in combat. Even Hotspur (that self-declared Philistine who hates 'mincing poetry') might well appreciate it. For Hotspur is moved by Shakespeare to show comparable ardour when he vows himself ready to leap to the moon or dive to the bottom of the deep in his quest for honour.

It may be thought that Falstaff is of course an old fraud who does not really mean what he says when he engages in praise of valour and that by contrast Hotspur very naïvely means just what he says in praise of it. Likewise it may be thought that when Falstaff in his more famous soliloquy rejects honour as no more than an airy word and scorns the death-defying valour it demands from a combatant, he is obviously a sensible realist and means just what he says. To think thus is to think that where Shakespeare has presented doubleness in Falstaff we are challenged to discover in which part of him lies the Simon-Pure Falstaff. That way peril lies. Whenever one finds Falstaff to be double one must beware of diminishing his grotesqueness—and losing him—by discarding something of him. Falstaff can be a trap for his dramatic associates in the two parts of *Henry IV*, and for us too he can be a trap. It is not only by tempting us to make a neat yes or no decision on whether he is a coward that he can trap us.

Support that Falstaff as a praiser of sack gives to valour is grotesque to the full in the Falstaffian manner, and hence it both joins with and opposes such non-grotesque support as Hotspur and the reformed Prince provide. The toper's valour eulogized by Falstaff is not to be counted as high courage, but nevertheless in the soliloquy on sack Shakespeare has taken pains to win acceptance for Falstaff as a true admirer of valour according to his lights. He has given us ground to believe without any question whatever that Falstaff means wholeheartedly what he says when he begins by praising sack for helping the mind of man (his own surely included) to create delectable shapes imaginatively and excellent wit verbally. And it is plain that he would lead us on from our acceptance of wholeheartedness in Falstaff here at the outset of his sack-praising to an acceptance of honest feeling in him at its climax when the sack that has been made the cause of valour generally in mankind is more particularly made its cause in the 'very hot and valiant' reformed Prince. At that point Shakespeare goes so far as to touch our hearts for Falstaff's benefit by making praise of the valiant Prince, whom Falstaff regards himself as having nurtured, lead to a revelation in Falstaff of the instincts of a grotesque father: 'If I had a thousand sons, the first humane principle I would teach them should be to forswear thin potations and addict themselves to sack.' It follows that the very modern suggestion can be made, as it is made by J. I. M. Stewart, that in ascending to the kingship the Prince 'kills Falstaff instead of killing the king, his father', since in a sense 'Falstaff *is* his father; certainly is a "father-substitute" in the psychologist's word'.[1]

Though Falstaff the generous drinker of sack makes no claim to possession of a fierce courage, Falstaff the animal-man offers an image of himself as a predator. He does so with a strangely becoming modesty. As he plans what he is to do to Justice Shallow he is in his own eyes not a beast of prey such as a lion, or a bird of prey such as a hawk. He is not a rapacious creature high enough in nature's scheme to be counted noble by the nobly combative among the non-grotesque. With grotesque aptness he is a fish of prey, and his victim is a foolish fishling: 'If the young dace be a bait for the old pike, I see no reason in the law of nature but I may snap at him' (*2 Henry IV*, III. ii. 356–8).

In connection with the grotesque support Falstaff gives to the combative honour that makes warfare a major pursuit it is revealing to look at the form he takes as not an ordinary Vice but one for whom war is his element. For he follows the wars in a manner that was developed within a part of the Vice tradition that Shakespeare shows he knew. When Falstaff prepares for acting the part of the Prince's father in the mock interview scene and says he will do it 'in King Cambyses' vein' (*1 Henry IV*, II. iv. 427), there is no reason to doubt that Shakespeare has in mind Thomas Preston's *Cambises* (entered in 1569 and printed without date). Through Falstaff Shakespeare is having sport with an old pretentiousness of dramatic high style in that play. But in making Falstaff allude thus to *Cambises* he does more than point back to passages

---

[1] *Character and Motive in Shakespeare*, London, 1949, p. 138.

of attempted high seriousness in that play alone.[1] Among other plays to which he may be said to draw attention is a morality I have mentioned in my first chapter as being very similar in cast to *Cambises* and of the same early Elizabethan period. This is John Pickering's *Horestes* (printed in 1567). It not only has passages of high style 'in King Cambyses' vein' but like *Cambises* has a Vice that takes the form of a soldier of fortune.

Cambises and *Horestes*, as I have said, are examples of what may be called the morality-tragedy. They look forward to forms of tragedy and chronicle-history drama established on the later Elizabethan stage.[2] The first play dramatizes a Renaissance account of the reign of Cambyses, King of Persia, and the second a medieval version of the Orestes saga, and each puts into its classical setting a Vice who brings about or rejoices in subversion of virtue among the high but welcomes opportunities to turn his attentions to the low. This Vice goes to war because the hero goes to war and also because he enjoys strife in any form, among the low as well as among the high. The hero goes to war because he desires to 'proceed in virtuous life' according to the code of combative honour, as Cambises is urged to do at the beginning of his reign by a councillor who might, in good morality fashion, have been named Wisdom. For Cambises the pursuit of honour is the conquering of Egypt and for Horestes it is the taking of revenge for his father's murder.

The Vice in each play has doublenesses that resemble to a certain extent the much subtler ones in Falstaff. In *Cambises* his name, aptly enough, is Ambidexter and he says he has it because he 'plays with both hands'. As he elaborates his meaning and demonstrates his ability, it develops that he has many kinds of ambidexterity. For example he can be double by deceitfully seeming what he is not or even by doing good as well as evil. In *Horestes* the Vice is

---

[1] For indications that *Cambises* was a 'stock joke' and was made to stand for a stylistic trend see an appendix contributed by J. C. Maxwell to the Arden Shakespeare *1 Henry IV*, ed. A. R. Humphreys, London, 1960, pp. 199–200.

[2] The contribution of these morality-tragedies to the shaping of Elizabethan tragedy I have discussed at some length in *The Medieval Heritage of Elizabethan Tragedy*, Berkeley, 1936, pp. 258 ff.

not so variously double. He deceives, of course, and practises an old trick of his kind by taking at will a virtuous name to cover his vicious quality. To deceive his low companions he calls himself Patience. To deceive Horestes he puts himself on the side of honour by saying that his name is Courage and that he has come as a messenger from the gods to announce that Horestes must take revenge for his father's murder. At the end of the play he changes his name to Revenge to mark the success he has had, but he bewails the fact that he is now rejected and must go begging because Horestes no longer needs Revenge. There seems to be confusion as to whether the taking of revenge is here a sin for Horestes that is nurtured by the Vice or is a true deed of honour for Horestes brought about deviously by the Vice to provide for himself the pleasure of seeing strife and bloodshed produced by the execution of justice. Pickering's quality as a dramatist in general does not invite the thought that he tries subtly to show the very concept of revenge for honour as having aspects of both good and evil.

A doubleness given to Preston's Vice and Pickering's that resembles with great particularity a doubleness in Falstaff is that which displays on one side a fascination with combat and an urge to enter into it, even with some daring, and on the other side a fascination with staying alive and an urge to keep escape routes from combat always open. Ambidexter and Patience–Courage–Revenge are almost as ambidextrous as Falstaff in ability either to accept or reject a fight. Each can justify rejection of a fight with a wise saw, just as Falstaff can. Says Ambidexter, laughing at himself after avoiding a fight:

It is wisdome (quoth I) by the masse, to save one.[1]

Says Patience–Courage–Revenge, after swallowing what he takes to be a slight upon his honour made when a country clown has misheard his name of Patience as Past Shame:

Good slepinge in a hole skynne, ould foulkes do saye.[2]

[1] *Cambises*, ed. John S. Farmer, Tudor Facsimile Reprints, London, 1910, sig. B4.
[2] *Horestes*, ed. Daniel Seltzer, Malone Society Reprints, Oxford, 1962, l. 117.

And says Falstaff, who is just as obviously past shame as he rises up from feigning death after being bested in his fight with Douglas: 'The better part of valour is discretion; in the which better part I have saved my life' (*1 Henry IV*, v. iv. 118–19).

5

Falstaff makes his contribution to the theme of conscience in the two parts of *Henry IV* by declaring and proving that he does not have any conscience. He has no prickings within to bother him when he goes against established codes of action. When the Prince prepares to hear the complaint of the Sheriff after the Gadshill robbery and says, 'Now, my masters, for a true face and a good conscience', Falstaff replies matter-of-factly, 'Both which I have had; but their date is out, and therefore I'll hide me.' It is an animal-like lack of both good and bad conscience that can allow him to fall asleep behind the arras and be found, 'snorting like a horse' when the Sheriff is gone. This monstrous lack of something proper to man's more-than-animal state outdoes a monstrous lack of man's proper staff of life in Falstaff's diet that is revealed by papers rifled from his pockets while he is asleep. Upon what is charged to him there as part of a supper the Prince makes the comment: 'O monstrous! but one halfpennyworth of bread to this intolerable deal of sack!' (*1 Henry IV*, ii. iv. 589–90.)

It may at first appear that in *The Merry Wives of Windsor* Falstaff is at last given a conscience. Certainly in the final scene of that play he comes to feel shame that he has not known before and fails for the first time to rise triumphantly above disgrace. But this shame of his proves upon examination to be different indeed from shame over wrongdoing. It is shame over a lack of cleverness in perceiving and doing. The lack is one that he has never thought himself capable of, any more than we have thought him capable of it after following him through *Henry IV*. He is completely 'dejected' because he has been 'made an ass' and because he has 'liv'd to stand at the taunt' of a Welsh parson, 'one that makes fritters of English'. When he wonders whether he has laid his brain 'in the sun, and dried it', and concludes that degradation he has come to experience 'is enough to be the decay of lust and late-walking through the realm', he must be taken to mean that what he is called upon to do is not to repent and follow virtue but to regain his knowingness and thus counter any further threat to his untrammelled way of life.

The consciencelessness of Falstaff thus preserves itself even while he is in many ways transformed in *The Merry Wives*. It is elementally strong. The animal man in Falstaff is domesticated, but it insists upon living according to codes of its own. Falstaff is less bound to humanity around him than is the dog that has a master, though the Prince does compare his familiarity with a dog's. Along with the animal man in him there is also the Vice to give an aspect of inevitability to his consciencelessness. These two of the Falstaffian components lend strength to each other.

The morality Vice from whom Falstaff inherits, who is both a Vice that follows the hero in war, as in *Cambises* and *Horestes*, and a Vice with whom the hero goes roistering in taverns, as in some other plays, can be so much at one with the animal nature in man that he merges with it. For the Vice of the morality play, as seems to be plain, is an unregenerate quality in mankind, striving to undo humanity from within instead of being a diabolic force working upon it from without, though of course he can consort with devils. If the Vice is called Sensuality, as, for example, in Henry Medwall's *Nature* (written at the end of the fifteenth century), he can be recognized as having a just claim upon man because he is a natural part of him. But he is a dangerous lower part and must be ruled by a higher part, that is, by Reason, who has his place in man because man is 'halfe angelyke'. In *Nature* even Nature herself gives to Man a warning against being too much the creature of nature:

> I wot well sensualyte / ys to the naturall
> And graunted to the / in thy furst creacyon
> But not wythstandyng / yt ought to be ouerall
> Subdued to reason / and vnder hys tuycyon.[1]

---

[1] *Nature*, ed. Alois Brandl, *Quellen des weltlichen Dramas in England vor Shakespeare*, Strassburg, 1898, pp. 75–158, ll. 162–5.

Inevitably Man in this play falls before temptation, leaves Reason, and lets Sensuality introduce him to Falstaffian delinquency in the tavern before he gives due heed to the angelic within him.

But, compared with Ambidexter in *Cambises* and Patience–Courage–Revenge in *Horestes*, this Sensuality in *Nature* reveals a lack of verve in his creator. One should be charitable to Medwall and remember that he wrote *Nature* more than half a century before the other two plays were written and that in the intervening time there was a rising tide of dramatic and other development within the Renaissance from which the authors of these later plays benefited. A great difference between Sensuality and the Vices in *Cambises* and *Horestes* is that he is weighed down with responsibility, first for arguing his rights in man and then for making man exclusively his own, while they are unburdened and have a vivacity of some appeal both as speakers and doers. They have an elfin quality. They are Puckish. They do man harm or benefit him indifferently and according to whim, and thus they take the natural in man into a relationship with essences of nature such as are traditionally represented by the realm of faerie. Ambidexter particularly is given an elfin cast as he attends upon both the doing of good and the doing of evil and as he takes mischievous pleasure in their mixture within the worldly scheme of things.

Ironically the grossly fat Falstaff also has a side that is elfin. It is a side without which he could not have the strong appeal he does have. He makes the most of it, so much so that he becomes more ingratiating than an Ambidexter and more engaging than a Puck. One thing he reveals which always works favourably upon our feelings is a natural amiability. He is utterly conscienceless but not intrinsically cruel. He preys upon the Hostess or Justice Shallow, not because he delights in causing them pain, but because he delights in getting from them what cries out to be transferred to himself. Moreover, in a way most striking he lacks anything at all of the deep-set mischievous quality of an Ambidexter or a Puck. He does not foment cat-and-dog fights among persons around him. And it redounds greatly to his credit that though he is cruelly tricked by the Prince, first as he trustingly engages with him in highway robbery and later as he takes an evening's ease with Doll Tearsheet, yet he never descends to playing practical jokes, in the way of retaliation or otherwise. He does not even play them on a person so defenceless as the drawer Francis, whom the Prince victimizes with no compunction at all.

At the end of *The Merry Wives of Windsor* the elfin Falstaff suffers the climactic indignity of being offered up for judgement to a troop of provincials in fairy disguises. But in *Henry V* the sending of him after death to 'Arthur's bosom'—to some grotesque Elysium in Avalon where his 'fracted and corroborate' heart can undergo faerie healing—is a malapropistic inspiration on the part of the Hostess that gives him his due.

IV

HAMLET AMONG FOOLS

1

As *Hamlet* raises its many questions it shows notable capacity to raise questions about the Shakespearean grotesque. Voltaire for one can help us to realize that capacity. Voltaire, of course, was of his age as well as for all time and it was only too easy for him to find the Shakespearean grotesque repellent. Yet we benefit by what he says against it. It does not matter how radically we disagree with him as dwellers in an age when acceptance of the grotesque in an earlier form is natural because of what the grotesque means to us in our own form. When Voltaire condemns the grotesque in Shakespeare, and especially that in *Hamlet*, as an outrage against artistic and general decency, he helps us to know the substance of it. He can save us from taking it too much for granted.

He can even be helpful when he objects to that rather engaging remark of Francisco's in the opening lines of *Hamlet*: 'Not a mouse stirring.' I suppose that what Francisco says here arouses no very strong aversion now. We perhaps let ourselves feel a modern superiority when we find that Voltaire rebukes Shakespeare for making Francisco bring a bit of jocosity out of the mouths of the folk into a tragedy of high pretensions. Voltaire thinks that in a guardhouse, among his base fellows, a soldier might talk thus about having had a quiet guard, but he maintains that an author has no business making a player soldier do so in a theatre before a cultivated audience used to expressing itself nobly.[1] We may do well not to pass this argument by too quickly. It is helpful, for example, to consider an answer to it given in England by Thomas

---

[1] See *Collection Complette des Œuvres de Mr de Voltaire*, Geneva, 1768–77, xxx. 517–18.

H

Davies, very much a lesser man of the eighteenth century, who makes an excellent foil for Voltaire. By attempting to overthrow him Davies elevates Voltaire in our estimation. 'But', says he of Francisco's unabashed mention of the mouse, 'could there be a properer mode of describing the solitariness which reigned in the place, than by saying that everything was so still that the soft tread of a small reptile had not been heard? The insignificance of an object does by no means lessen the general idea. Have not the most celebrated antient dramatic writers admitted thoughts as low, and words more gross and offensive into their best trage-dies?'

As a defender of Shakespeare Davies is fighting on 'proper' ground that we now think cannot be held and he is calling up most dubious aid from the troops of the ancients. Voltaire has a good deal the better of the solemn Davies because he knows at least that Francisco's mouse is an antic detail that has a Gothic, not an ancient classic, quality. For him it is therefore unacceptable. He says scornfully that what we have to deal with here is a *quolibet d'un soldat* wholly out of place. We, from our lack of scorn, may reply that this is truly enough a soldier's *quolibet* but that it is well placed as a touch of grotesqueness in the midst of the seriousness and intensity that attend the coming of a royal ghost. It is offered by a guardsman who can be thought to know perfectly well what it is to have fear of the awe-inspiring but who for the moment treats fear irreverently, though without making the silly boast that he is not fearful. Yet no matter how natural Francisco has been made to seem, there is no need to talk about a satisfying 'realism' provided by a common soldier if one would get down to something essential. And no matter how much this soldier may lack nobility or how much the scene in which he appears may create tension in an audience, there is no essential need to talk about a satisfying 'comic relief'. What matters most is that Shake-speare through Francisco makes one know, by a touch however light, that the non-grotesque may do more than merely escape

---

[1] *Dramatic Micellanies* [sic]: *Consisting of Critical Observations on Several Plays of Shakespeare*, London, 1784, iii. 6.

weakening when the grotesque joins with it while remaining ostensibly adverse. It may even grow stronger.

The reason does not always, by any means, appear to be that the non-grotesque can develop for itself an added power with which to meet the challenge of the grotesque. Often enough it seems to be that the non-grotesque can draw supporting power from the grotesque to which it is joined and that it can do so because in the grotesque there is frequently an antic satisfaction taken in the very existence of the non-grotesque. This can even be a well-wishing joy, such as a court fool may have that there is majesty to which he may be conjoined for the health of both majesty and folly. About well-wishing for a king which is supremely strong in Lear's fool I will say something later. In the meanwhile, it is enough to say that Francisco, for a brief moment at the beginning of *Hamlet*, has grotesque validity as a jester showing profound sympathy for royalty he jests about. It is the dead King Hamlet, who on the two preceding nights has appeared as a ghost, that is the subject of his jesting. That Francisco is deeply moved because he fears all is not well with the ghost and with the kingdom and that he offers his jest wryly is made plain. He has just said he has felt discomfort from more than the bitter coldness of the night. He has been 'sick at heart'.

2

In *Hamlet* the joining of the grotesque with the non-grotesque is such that Voltairean fastidiousness has grounds enough, according to its lights, for finding that the grotesque has here been most viciously intrusive. Hamlet himself may be said to be so deeply invaded by the grotesque that he has a double nature, a nature in which a prince and a court fool share alike. In *Henry IV* there is no comparable invasion of the hero by the grotesque. Just as Hal the prince dominates and looks down upon Falstaff as he cultivates him for amusement, so does he hold in subjection Hal the truant and jester.

Grotesqueness established within Hamlet presumes constantly to offer him a challenging vision. It is a vision of the human state of being and of his own position in the setting of life on earth. At times it is a vision reminiscent of the figure of naked mankind presented as pushing his way through a thicket of tangled coils in a medieval manuscript illumination. When Hamlet responds by speaking of what is thus put before his mind's eye, he shows that the Shakespearean grotesque has come to have force and subtlety greater than it has in *Henry IV*. The new force and subtlety are manifest both when grotesqueness is that of man taken as showing naked animality and when it is that of man or man's surrounding world taken as showing monstrosity.

Newness of Shakespearean conception is most striking when its theme is monstrosity, and not only if comparison is made with what has already been found of that theme in *Henry IV*. I now turn to a consideration of the theme as it appears in *Julius Caesar*, the tragedy which according to general opinion immediately precedes *Hamlet*. I do so in order to make a contrast between what is done with the theme there, in one tragic context, and what is done with it soon afterward in another, in *Hamlet*.

What is not comic in the monstrous may be so far from comic that it inspires awe of a kind deeply rooted in man's past. In *Julius Caesar* Shakespeare names and uses awe-inspiring monstrosity of an old order of conception when he makes prodigies 'conjointly meet' to foreshadow catastrophe and has Cassius answer the question

> Why all these things change from their ordinance,
> Their natures, and preformed faculties,
> To monstrous quality

by saying that

> heaven hath infus'd them with these spirits
> To make them instruments of fear and warning
> Unto some monstrous state

$$(\text{I. iii. } 66\text{--}71).$$

That which Cassius is made to say here is in keeping with other things in the play which give it a characteristic direction in its exploration of moral man and his universe. With Cassius the monstrous is truly *monstrosus* in an ancient sense. Thus for him the monster can be the original *monstrum*, the evil omen, the divine warning. Also, it can be something that is not fearfully supernatural but horribly unnatural because of a nefarious departure from right being. His argument is that the commonwealth of Rome has come to a monstrous condition (has left the path of nature in its drift toward Caesarism) and needs to be divinely threatened by monstrous signs (events that do not belong in nature). In both of these senses what is monstrous raises qualms in the observer because it presents a problem of disorder in man's natural surroundings. There is no way implied of accepting this disorder in nature with any peace of mind. When caused by man it angers divinity. When caused by divinity it terrifies man—quite properly, for man must learn how to placate divinity by removing the disorder he causes and thus get divinity to remove the retaliatory disorder *it* causes.

Cassius has found portents, and he interprets them according to his views or, rather, according to his special interests. If he is thus made to have a theology and a philosophy not to be thought of as entirely honest, he is nevertheless made to set the key for the theme of the monstrous found in the play. Brutus, whose thinking is all too simply honest, accords with Cassius in seeing the monstrous as a horrifying departure from natural rightness. But for him, very unsimply because fate deals with him ironically, what appears to be horribly unnatural is something that must be done *for* Rome to save it in the future, not something already done *to* Rome that now makes saving it necessary. With Caesar in power Rome could be eventually monstrous. Only conspiracy can destroy the possibility of its being monstrous. But conspiracy itself is monstrous, even in a good cause. It is doubly monstrous when its good cause is the assassination of a man like Caesar just because he might possibly be corrupted by too much power. Such conspiracy must go skulking even by night, 'when evils are most free', and Brutus asks of it:

> O, then by day
> Where wilt thou find a cavern dark enough
> To mask thy monstrous visage? (ɪɪ. i. 79–81.)

After conspiracy has had its way with Caesar, Brutus comes to know that he is part of a preternatural monstrosity that must produce as reaction a supernatural monstrosity. In the end he perceives fully the rightness of Caesar's ghost in the scheme of things. He cannot dispose of the 'monstrous apparition' by laying it to the 'weakness' of his eyes, as he tries to do.

The extent to which the monstrosity that is tragedy for Brutus is for him separated from comedy is one measure of the marked difference between *Julius Caesar* and *Hamlet*. The difference is all the more significant in that there is also a marked likeness between the two tragedies: each presents idealism which with conscientious misgivings accepts a duty of assassination and which fails profoundly to attain its end, though it succeeds superficially by disposing of its victim. Tragedy with this particular moral involution Shakespeare did not attempt again, but he made these two versions of it within a period of a year or two. And the second of them, *Hamlet*, suddenly achieved a much more profound drama of civilized contentions within the human spirit than the first. Hamlet's speculations when he has doubts about a ghost are not like anything so unpsychological as Brutus' thought that he has weak eyes. Also, the impulse that develops in Hamlet to lay a ghost in sophisticated fashion by subjecting it to oblivion is like nothing at all in Brutus. Hamlet's courses of feeling, thought, and action are so unsimple to our eyes that we easily make him a mystery of the kind we make our baffling selves. Always near the centre of the Hamlet mystery is the grotesque, strong in the dramatic construction of Hamlet himself. The dominant spirit of this grotesque is that of the wry jest. For Hamlet his state of existence draws on toward being infinitely comical though infinitely distressing. Brutus is not made able to see his haunting ghost in any guise that reminds us even remotely of Hamlet's 'old mole', a spirit that is incongruously an animal burrower in the clogging non-spiritual medium of earth. Indeed Brutus is quite given over to a painfully earnest gravity and does not even attempt the agonized jesting in earnest without which Hamlet would not be Hamlet. Thus Shakespeare provides Brutus with no Polonius to work upon and no gravedigger to work with. He gives him no inner sense of, and no outer support from, the grotesquely comic. Grotesquery yielded by Roman citizens has its part in the play but to Brutus it is made to mean nothing whatever.

In *Hamlet* the words 'monster' and 'monstrous' are never used as they are in *Julius Caesar*. They never mean that something is awe-inspiring as a divine warning or horrible as a visitation for mankind. The ghost of the elder Hamlet is an 'apparition' and a 'dreaded sight', it 'bodes some strange eruption' to the state, and it works supernaturally against the doer of a most unnatural crime, but what it is and what has brought about its coming we do not hear of as being monstrous.

Moreover, in *Hamlet* designated monstrosity has a complex quality it does not have in *Julius Caesar*, or in any other earlier play of Shakespeare's. Fittingly enough Shakespeare makes Hamlet himself responsible for presenting this complexity. It comes from incongruity, sometimes of more than one kind, between parts of an imaged monster as well as between the monster as a whole and whatever may be regarded as having the natural form that the monster lacks. The latter sort of incongruity, which produces the general idea of deformity, is of course essential where there is to be any concept of monstrosity at all. In *Julius Caesar* the dramatic quality of monstrosity comes only from this incongruity between the monstrous and something other than the monstrous. But in *Hamlet* there is always incongruity within the monstrous itself, and it is put before us by Hamlet in a way that is made characteristic of his imagination.

There are three images of monsters that Hamlet is made to create and to label as what they are. The first is that of the player who so forces his soul to his own 'conceit' that for a 'fiction'—for Hecuba—he sheds tears and shows otherwise the bodily effects of grief (II. ii. 577–84). Hamlet asks whether what is found here is not 'monstrous', and he does so not merely because of the incongruity between this unnatural man who weeps 'all for nothing' and the natural man who weeps only for something. He looks further and sees within the weeping player incongruities that are even more monstrous. These occur between pairs of entities that are made to defy natural separateness and achieve strangely effective oneness. In his 'dream of passion' the player brings into such oneness the world of imaginative experience and the world of ordinary experience, so that his tears and changes of expression are as honest as those of any witness sympathizing with a living Hecuba in her misfortune. They are not put on. Things naturally distinct that the player unites within himself are the opposites commonly called unreality and reality. What is formed as a result is an admirable monster in which untruth and truth come together to make poetic truth, or for the actor dramatic truth. The actor's art goes beyond nature in creation.

The second of Hamlet's designated monsters takes form in the course of his 'get thee to a nunnery' injunction to Ophelia. It does so in these words: 'Or if thou wilt needs marry, marry a fool; for wise men know well enough what monsters you make of them' (III. i. 143–6). The context makes it apparent that we do not come to know Hamlet's concept of monstrosity in this instance merely by calling to mind an observation made by the tortured Othello when he thinks of himself as a cuckolded husband wearing horns:

> A horned man's a monster and a beast
> (*Othello*, IV. i. 63).

Hamlet can find a depth of unfaithfulness in woman, but here he is not doing only that. If we look back upon the development of the nunnery speech, we see that Shakespeare has once again set Hamlet's imagination to work upon pairing incongruous things. To begin with they are honesty and susceptible beauty in women ('your honesty should admit no discourse to your beauty'), matched by virtue and arrant knavery in men ('virtue cannot so inoculate our old stock but we shall relish of it'). By extension he comes to consider incongruity between, instead of within, women and men. In this way he arrives at the advice he gives Ophelia to marry a fool, not a wise man, if she must marry. For a woman has various empty-headed follies that make the wise man who is married to her into a monster, and Hamlet gives a catalogue of them. Hence the monster may be seen as created thus: a wise man becomes a fool by marrying a foolish woman in the first place, and married life with her, especially if he is uxorious, confirms him in folly of which his wisdom is always conscious, so that she by her folly makes him into a consciously absurd figure of wisdom–folly; in this way he becomes a double-bodied monster. Hamlet concludes by dramatizing himself as having gone mad thinking of such a man's plight as he declares: 'I say, we will have no more marriages.'

When we come to the last of Hamlet's designated monsters, we find a figure in which opposites no less great than folly and wisdom are even more intricately united. They are good and evil. This figure is presented in the lines by which Hamlet urges his mother to avoid his uncle's bed and to 'live the purer':

> That monster, custom, who all sense doth eat,
> Of habits devil, is angel yet in this,
> That to the use of actions fair and good
> He likewise gives a frock or livery
> That aptly is put on
>
> (III. iv. 161–5).

The passage shows custom as a monster that eats—or feeds upon, or takes life from—all human sense, not only bodily sense but also mental and spiritual sense. Custom is both evil and good, just as human sense serves and becomes both evil and good. Of habits—i.e. in respect of habits—custom is a devil and is also an angel. Habits make it biform. But the word 'habits' is itself biform. It means in one way settled practices and in another way suitable garb such as 'a frock or livery'. Thus it makes intricate the way in which opposites within the figure of custom are joined.[1]

---

[1] The interpretation offered does not depend upon emendation. The passage, which is omitted in the folio of 1623, is given here with the wording of the quarto of 1604–5. No change in that wording is called for to give the passage meaning. Upon 'sense' as meaning the 'outward' senses viewed as a single bodily faculty and also meaning the 'inner' faculties of mind and soul, and upon 'of' as meaning 'in respect of', see 'Sense' and 'Of' in the *Oxford English Dictionary*. The emendation

In this word 'habits', as Hamlet works upon it for his mother's spiritual benefit, we meet a pun as deserving of the name of monster as 'that monster custom' on which its existence depends. In its dramatic setting it deserves to be called a grimly comic, rather than an 'uncomic', pun. It shows an unseemly joy taken in witty contrivance of expression that has before been made characteristic of the speaker at times of most earnest intensity. It does not startle as the word-play of Laertes does when he forbids himself tears for the drowned Ophelia and says he does so because she already has 'too much of water' (IV. vii. 187). In that case it is left for Shakespeare alone, standing out from behind his Laertes, to plead joy of contrivance. The doubleness in the word 'water', with its monstrous incongruity between the animosity in streams that drown and the sympathy in tears that mourn the drowning, is clearly uncalled for from the straightforward Laertes. But the grotesque imagination given to Hamlet makes touching or dwelling upon incongruity such as this always in order for him. He is chief of all players with words in Shakespeare's plays.[1]

3

For Hamlet the supreme monster in a world productive of monstrosity is man, though he never gives the name to him. Hamlet's basic vision of man is of a double being, in one part godlike, or angelic, and 'noble in reason', in the other part ignoble and merely 'quintessence of dust', like the beast that perishes, the beast that 'wants discourse of reason'. Man in this vision is raised gratifyingly far above the beast, but with the reason he thus acquires he cannot escape seeing that his highness remains bound to an animal lowness and that this lowness, in relation to his highness,

---

that changes 'Of habits devil' into 'Of habits evil' and makes the immediately preceding words, 'who all sense doth eat', mean a killing by custom of all moral realization with regard to the evil habits, is a way to get rid of the monstrous devil–angel union that forms the figure of custom. But a vaguely monstrous combination of evil and good propensities which then insists on remaining within the figure shows that the change is only a weakening of it.

[1] See M. M. Mahood, *Shakespeare's Wordplay*, London, 1957, p. 166.

is grotesque. The perception thus given to Hamlet affects strongly
the imagery of the play.

For example, *Hamlet* stands by itself when compared for animal
imagery with three other mature tragedies of Shakespeare's with
which it is often associated: *Othello*, *King Lear*, and *Macbeth*. In
these there is much animal imagery which reflects viciousness
shown by man and which reinforces the emotional effect of
resultant human suffering, suffering that is brought about wan-
tonly, predatorily, ferociously, or in the direst way of evil. *King
Lear*, as criticism has amply demonstrated, shows the most intense
use of such animal imagery. In contrast *Hamlet* is remarkable for
infrequent use of it and for the feeling given that what use actually
is made contributes little to the tragic essence of the play. Absent
from the poetry of *Hamlet* are the wolf and the bear, though they
form images in the other three tragedies and though they come
easily to Shakespeare's mind as expressions of vicious nature. One
thinks of the grouping of the two in the oxymorons that Timon,
when he serves his mock banquet, hurls at the perfidious friends
who have preyed upon him: 'affable wolves, meek bears' (*Timon
of Athens*, III. vi. 105). The tiger, whose viciousness is in Lear's
daughters, does make one appearance in *Hamlet* but, significantly,
this is at such a remove from the mainstream of the drama that it
comes when Pyrrhus is likened to 'th' Hyrcanian beast' in Hamlet's false beginning of a speech on Priam's slaughter from a play
possessed by the visiting actors (II. ii. 472). In this speech the
imagery has a histrionic grandiloquence that sets it off from
imagery in the drama proper. There the only animal images that
present viciousness like that of the wolf, the bear, or the tiger are
serpent images. One of these comes from the ghost of Hamlet's
father and makes of Claudius an 'adulterate beast', a 'serpent' who
has stung his brother's life and now enjoys the victim's crown and
his queen (I. v. 39–42). The other comes from Hamlet and likens
Rosencrantz and Guildenstern to 'adders fang'd' that are not to be
trusted (III. iv. 203). There is an image in which Hamlet, when he
breaks away from his companions to follow and speak to the
ghost, finds each petty artery in his body 'as hardy as the Nemean

lion's nerve'. But here the lion has the aspect of nobility which often prevails over its aspect as a savage beast of prey.[1]

A consideration of the various ways in which Hamlet sees something of the animal in himself is revealing. We have just found him comparing himself for extreme courageousness with a lion that only Hercules could conquer. In this comparison he is made to show a romantic animalitarianism. That kind of thing, unrelieved and unequivocal, he does not fall into again as he characterizes his own qualities. He is equivocal in the scene where he struggles with Laertes in Ophelia's grave. Reproaching Laertes for an ill return made in response to loving-kindness he concludes thus:

> Let Hercules himself do what he may,
> The cat will mew, and dog will have his day
>   (v. i. 314–15).

Here it may be either Laertes or Hamlet that is meant to be of cat and dog status. But, for reasons that appear when we look further into what Hamlet does with himself in animal comparisons, we may find it the more fitting to think that he is taking as his own the place of creatures as lowly but as adequate as the cat and dog. In their adequacy these can even scorn a lion-killing Hercules, who cannot suppress them or keep them from being what they are. They will get their innings. Let Laertes be Hercules. Or, for that matter, let the King be Hercules too. But the Hamlet who would thus make himself cat or dog in challenging a Hercules would most certainly be an ironic Hamlet, not ranking himself in all simplicity with cats and dogs any more than with gravediggers. He would take delight in the grotesque truth that in Hamlet the Dane, as he announces himself in princely style when he leaps into the grave to grapple with Laertes, there is a very effective cat or dog

---

[1] Probably because she finds other imagery dominant in *Hamlet*, Caroline F. E. Spurgeon, in *Shakespeare's Imagery*, Cambridge, 1935, neglects the animal imagery in the play except in a listing of its images in general in her Appendix IV, p. 368. What she says briefly on the effect of animal imagery in *Macbeth*, p. 334, and *Othello* and *King Lear*, p. 336, is helpful.

in the same sense that there is in him a very effective gravedigger
who is a matcher of knavish wits with the most absolute knave
of a gravedigger that can be found. Hamlet shows recurrently
a lively understanding that high and low thus join within him
monstrously.

Aside from his lapse into comparing himself with the Nemean
lion, Hamlet, when he thinks of himself in animal terms, always
does something similar to what he can be interpreted as doing
with the cat and dog. He plays himself down and does so by bringing the domestic or the humbler animals into his self-portrait. Yet
he never gives the impression that in comparisons of himself with
them he is forgetting that he is the princely Hamlet. Such comparisons he finds intriguing and often diverting because they have
truth and not-truth in them in a way beyond that of the ordinary
comparison. The Hamlet ego, which we can wish lessened only
if we wish to get rid of the essential Hamlet drama, makes for a
special tension between things bound together in these findings of
likenesses. One result of this is pleasure taken in the grotesque by
any follower of the play who has sympathetically entered into its
spirit. To Rosencrantz and Guildenstern Hamlet implies, when
there is discussion of his lack of advancement to the kingship, that
he is a horse turned out to grass and is finding the grass in short
supply. He quotes the beginning of a proverb, 'While the grass
grows', and leaves understood the ending, 'the horse starves' (iii.
ii. 358). When they ask him to tell where the body of Polonius is
hid and to go with them to the King, he cries, as the scene ends,
'Hide fox, and all after' (iv. ii. 32–3). As to who the fox is in this
probable echo of a children's game of hide-and-seek, one need not
have much doubt. The indication is that Hamlet makes his exit
running away from Rosencrantz and Guildenstern like a madman,
challenging them to catch him if they would take him to the King.
Hamlet fancies himself in the guise of a lowly creature able to
scheme protectively against hostile schemers. When he tells Horatio how he has triumphantly met craft with craft in sending Rosencrantz and Guildenstern to death in England in place of himself, he
will have it understood that he is a fish that has been fished for but

not caught. The King has 'thrown out his angle' for his 'proper life' (v. ii. 66).

For Hamlet it is beguiling to see himself as beastlike in an excessively unheroic way, but at the same time it is painful, and sometimes the pain comes from sober recognition of the direction being taken by his tragedy. In the self-reproach of such recognition he plays himself down most fully. When the player who is moved to weep for Hecuba impels him to soliloquize upon his own lack of capacity to be moved to take vengeance for his father, he finds himself 'pigeon-liver'd' and an 'ass' (II. ii. 604–10). He also finds himself a 'stallion' (II. ii. 615). The word 'stallion' was applied in Shakespeare's time to a woman who was a prostitute or to either a man or a woman of generally lascivious life, and it was later, at least, given special application to a man who prostituted himself as a hired paramour. It comes from Hamlet as a climactic epithet after he has likened himself to a 'whore' and a 'drab' for the way he has basely failed in honourable doing and has turned to malediction. The word appears in the 'good' quarto of 1604–5 as 'stallyon'. Its counterpart in the folio of 1623 is 'scullion', which has been often accepted by editors but obviously does not suit so well the context of prostitution, however much virtue it may have in its relative lack of oddity for the present age.[1]

In the soliloquy that follows his meeting with Fortinbras—that 'delicate and tender prince' possessing a 'spirit with divine ambition puff'd' who dares all in his doing—Hamlet has his fullest realization of a monstrous complexity in mankind that has relation to his tragedy. Man is created to sleep and feed like a beast but not to make sleeping and eating his chief good. For man has 'godlike reason', which is of the spirit that makes him more than beast as well as beast, and he also has 'divine ambition', or aspiration, which is likewise of the spirit. Fortinbras makes aspiration his chief good. Just because he goes to war for an insignificant plot of land,

---

[1] See 'Stallion' in the *Oxford English Dictionary*, which gives the word as it occurs in the 1604–5 quarto of *Hamlet* as meaning courtesan. The *O.E.D.* queries whether the word in its application to a woman is not of an origin other than that it has in its application to a man. But the query is immaterial when one is concerned with the poetic effect of the word in *Hamlet* in the form given.

his ambition may seem to be paltry. But it has divine quality nevertheless in so far as honour is involved for him as a spiritual need. That need gives his aspiration such courage that his spirit

Makes mouths at the invisible event (IV. iv. 50).

In the light of what Fortinbras is and does Hamlet sees his own case in the following way. Like all men he undergoes having a doubleness in being beast and also more than beast, but unlike Fortinbras, certainly, he is perturbed by a subsidiary doubleness within the larger doubleness. This state of things is indicated when he considers whether his delay in avenging his father has been caused by

Bestial oblivion, or some craven scruple
Of thinking too precisely on th' event
(IV. iv. 40–1).

In his consideration of 'bestial oblivion' Hamlet acknowledges that what is beast in him may give itself naturally to thoughtless oblivion, to a forgetfulness of what the more-than-beast sets itself to remember. At this stage he recognizes the need of putting the more-than-beast that thinks and aspires into complete control of action demanded by honour. And the killing of Claudius is certainly so demanded. In his consideration of 'thinking too precisely on the event' Hamlet for purposes of argument gives the more-than-beast this complete control. But now he suddenly realizes that the more-than-beast has a disconcerting doubleness of its own. The reason and aspiration of which it is formed are no less capable of internecine warfare than are the beast and the more-than-beast within the whole man. Aspiration may say ardently: 'Yes, yes.' But reason may say thoughtfully: 'Maybe yes, maybe no.' At this stage he finds that his problem resists solution stubbornly.

Final solution is impossible for Hamlet, though at first he does not think so. For him, since reason is 'godlike' and aspiration is 'divine', the human spirit that is the more-than-beast has within it two sacred entities and each demands worship from him at the expense of the other. The choice between beast and more-than-beast is no sooner required of Hamlet in his thinking than he makes it. As between a lesser and a greater part of man, who would choose the lesser for rulership? (Hamlet is prominent among the Shakespearean supporters of hierarchism.) But how make the succeeding choice between the sacredness of reason and the sacredness of aspiration, both being of the highest? Fortinbras has chosen by letting aspiration quell reason. In one way the frustrated Hamlet envies him his resultant singleness of spirit. In another way he sees him as an unthinking fool. For if Hamlet knows the embarrassments of having reason, he also knows the incomparable and indisputable delights of having it. Whatever these delights, he resolves to desert reason if he must in order to do what he grants that he must. It is true that reason can be an 'excitement' of the spirit. It can show the need of and the way to honour for aspiring man. But it can also turn about and by argument make honour into an absurdity, and worse still it can by looking forward too precisely to consequences produce the craven scruple to quell honour's aspiration. At the close of his soliloquy Hamlet believes he is making a firm decision, after the manner of Fortinbras, to put out of his mind all thinking except what will further the honourable action to which he is dedicated:

> O, from this time forth,
> My thoughts be bloody, or be nothing worth!
>
> (IV. iv. 65–6.)

They cannot be. The climactic irony of the play is that when Hamlet actually kills the King, he does so planlessly, surprised by the occasion, impelled suddenly to action by the King's responsibility for the death that has just come to his mother and for his own death that is soon to come, saying to the King, 'follow my mother', but not even mentioning his father, to whose revenge he has dedicated and rededicated himself. And just before the end, when he tells Horatio about turning the King's writ of death away from himself and upon Rosencrantz and Guildenstern, we find him still engaged upon his old search for justification by

means of reason for killing the King: 'Is't not perfect conscience /
To quit him with this arm?' (v. ii. 67–8.)

At the very end Hamlet is, to a degree, still playing himself
down by presenting himself in animal terms:

> O, I die, Horatio!
> The potent poison quite o'ercrows my spirit
>
> (v. ii. 363–4).

The courage he finally takes credit for having is not the royal
courage of the Nemean lion. It is that of a gamecock that has
given its best in the cockpit but lies wounded to death, with an
opponent crowing over him. It is only fair to say that in the cockpit the spirit shown by a cock that dies truly game has its ardent
admirers. Nevertheless it is the courage of a creature little removed
from the barnyard, one of the humbler creatures still, no matter
how valorous. But we are not to forget that as Shakespeare brings
Hamlet to his end he gives him no lingering thought about the
possibility of his being a cock that is a craven. The Hamlet, who
with his reason can explore the 'craven scruple', can by 'special
providence' also find his way to a death by combat that satisfies
him as the opposite of cowardly, even though he does not forbear
to speak of it grotesquely.

4

The grotesque in the play gathers substance from Hamlet at the
same time that it draws to a point in him. This statement is peculiarly true with reference to Polonius when he is presented by
means of animal grotesquery. The self-esteemed arranger of
affairs who is made by Hamlet into 'so capital a calf' gives himself
the form of an animal-breeder in his scheming against Hamlet as
he says, 'I'll loose my daughter to him' (II. ii. 162). It is to be
remembered that when Polonius proposes the loosing of his
daughter, he concludes by saying the ruse must succeed, or

> Let me be no assistant for a state,
> But keep a farm and carters
>
> (II. ii. 166–7).

Polonius in his absurdities can sometimes remind us strangely of the stock rustic clown moving and having his say among his betters. In action-contrivance and in word-contrivance he is an unconsciously grotesque counterpart of the consciously grotesque in Hamlet. He has very obviously been given much of the beast to go with the modicum of reason which is as sacred and delightful to him as Hamlet's wealth of reason is to Hamlet. But he is of course oblivious of the calf in himself, while Hamlet is all too well aware of the fox in himself. Naturally Polonius is just as oblivious of beast-shapes in clouds which are to be seen with the eye of imagination, though he will diplomatically agree they are there if Hamlet says so. As for the thinking Polonius, with his indirections finding directions out and with his bait of falsehood catching the carp of truth, he is in one way a clownish echo of the thinking Hamlet but in another way a primitive version of that Hamlet, gratified with the first discovery of his reason and not carried far out of calfdom by understanding.

It is through Polonius the calf and Osric the chough that we know best the comic quality found by Hamlet in mankind when it shows the peculiar grotesqueness of helpless folly. Osric as well as Polonius may be said to play the part of a fool at the King's court. The King himself does not see these two as fools. He even respects them, and indeed we perceive that they are not fools in all ways. So far as they *are* fools, Hamlet is their appreciator. He supports them by practising foolery with them. Neither Polonius nor Osric knows himself to be a fool. Neither is 'wise enough to play the fool' with the understanding of Feste in *Twelfth Night*. Each as a fool is of course not a person of grossly deficient mentality such as the Elizabethans called a 'natural'. Yet for Hamlet each takes the place of such a natural fool in that each is a poor innocent, not knowing what goes on when sport is had at his expense and when he is led by the nose to reveal the pretentiousness of his scantily developed reason.

It is needful to be on guard when Hamlet implies that for him Polonius and Osric are absolute bores. We are not to take him simply at his word when he calls one a tedious old fool and the other a man whom it is a vice to know. The truth is, very plainly, that in a way they have a certain deep appeal for him, no matter how honestly he would hate to play the fool just as they do, all unconsciously. He delights to draw them out in their folly, know-ing that what the innocent fool does and says is unworked stuff of artistic foolery.

Both Polonius and Osric achieve much as fools that have each a large share of witlessness. They have high places instead of low at court. Polonius, whose witlessness is calflike in its bumbling, is a councillor giving advice to the King and passes as most wise. Osric, whose witlessness is choughlike, or crowlike, in its chatter-ing, eats at the King's table and is counted as among the flower of the gentry. On Osric Hamlet comments: 'He hath much land, and fertile: let a beast be lord of beasts, and his crib shall stand at the King's mess' (v. ii. 87–9). In him, as in Polonius, there is a monstrous grotesqueness of high joined with low. For some the monstrosity is hidden from sight. For Hamlet it therefore has in-creased attraction. By giving a sophisticatedly antic part of himself to Polonius and Osric as innocent antics Hamlet gives them further privileged standing in the entourage of royalty. He plays in his way the part of princely patron to them. He can look down upon them. He can be cruel to them. (The innocent fool in the great man's household could upon occasion have exceedingly heartless tricks played upon him.) But the satisfaction Hamlet takes in these two is quite often that of the rightly appreciative prince taken in the attendant fool.

A kind of foolery that Polonius and Osric do not achieve is that which matches wits with greatness and gives as good as it gets. This kind tends to be artful, not innocent, no matter how much it adopts the manner of the unknowing fool. Such foolery we find in someone who to Hamlet is also a beast of humble order, but with a difference. The sexton who throws up skulls as he digs Ophelia's grave is an 'ass'. Yet he is strangely capable when he comes up against the faculty of reason in a man like Hamlet. He is formidable in wit combat with Hamlet because he has for his part acquired a kind of reason which wilfully refuses to boast of being above animal nature and yet is a match for the reason which does boast thus. It stalks in beastly disguise the other reason as fair game. A skull subjected to being physically 'o'erreached' by the sexton brings from Hamlet the intimation in word-play that the skull's one-time possessor, who may have had limitless trust in the cleverness that reason had put into his head, is now bested in all his contrivance by an asinine rustic: 'This might be the pate of a politician, which this ass now o'erreaches; one that would circumvent God, might it not?' (v. i. 86–8.)[1] The speech has in it a fore-shadowing of the trouble Hamlet himself is to have to keep from being overreached by the wit of the grave-digging clown.

If Hamlet is not bested by the clown in wit combat, he is bested by him in another way and knows it. If he is not put down in his pride of reason, he is put down in another pride, in which he recognizes himself as utterly vulnerable. In medieval terms Hamlet is vulnerable in his pride of life. It is a pride that has been elevated by Renaissance visions of man's earthly glory but is shot through with Renaissance intellectual dubieties. And in medieval terms the clown with his spade does what the figure of Death does in the Dance of Death. The Dance traditionally has that figure as a human being already dead who points one of the living the way to the grave. In pictorial representation he is a decaying corpse or a skeleton who comes from the grave and calls, one by one, upon living figures ranging in rank from pope or emperor down to natural fool or innocent child, to prepare for death and follow him. The grave-digging clown in *Hamlet* takes the place of this corpse or skeleton. He occupies a grave he claims as his at the same time that he makes it for Ophelia. In it he is Death itself and from it he can speak to Hamlet of bodily dissolution with grotesque authority. To debate whether the grave he digs is his or Ophelia's is pointless. It belongs to him because it belongs to Everyman, alive or dead. The word-twisting that goes on over whether he 'lies' in the grave that he says is his and whether it is for the quick or the dead finally brings a riddling summons from the clown,

---

[1] The text of the quotation is that of the 'good' quarto of 1604–5. The folio of 1623 has 'o'er-offices' instead of 'o'erreaches'.

as Everyman–Death, to Hamlet, whose tragedy has drawn near to its ending in death: ' 'Tis a quick lie, sir; 'twill away again from me to you' (v. i. 139–40).

The skull of Yorick thrown up by the clown inevitably reminds Hamlet that death works king and jester, the non-grotesque and the grotesque, into a complete coming together to which any union of theirs in life has never brought them. In the Dance of Death the summoning corpse or skeleton wears no king's crown and no fool's dress, nor anything else to individualize it. It is truly Everyman dead, formed out of all men dead. At their earthly end there is the oneness of dust for the old King Hamlet and Yorick.

A fool, Hamlet perceives, is always a challenge to one who thinks himself beyond need to associate with a fool, and the ruler and the wise man are most open to the fool's challenge. Hamlet himself, who would be both ruler and wise man and has qualities of both, does not merely recognize the challenge to the full but accepts it to the full.

We need not ask whether Hamlet in his enjoyment of fools is meant to show all of that charity toward fools which St. Thomas More (himself a cherisher of a crazed household fool) credits to the Utopians: 'They take pleasure in fools. While they think it contemptible to mistreat them, they do not forbid men to enjoy their foolishness, and even regard this as beneficial to the fools.'[1] But we are not to miss, I should say, a true going out of Hamlet's spirit to the grave-digging clown and, more than to him, by much, to the dead Yorick as he is remembered. Hamlet's acceptance of the grotesquery for which Yorick has been responsible goes with love for the fool as well as love for his foolery. Thomas More would surely have approved.

5

In furtherance of the grotesque there are strange acceptances on the part of the non-grotesque, as Hamlet makes plain. There is the delighted acceptance by reason of the fool's anti-reason and

[1] *Utopia*, trans. and ed. H. S. V. Ogden, New York, 1949, p. 60.

the delighted acceptance by honour of the fool's anti-honour. Strangest of all for one concerned with imaginative art, there is the delighted acceptance by beauty of anti-beauty. All of these produce bondings of incongruities where discord remains even as mutual attraction becomes strong. They make centaur-like monsters of the kind that we have seen Shakespeare forming in Hamlet's imagination. The marriage of a wise man to a foolish woman and his delighting in her empty-headedness can produce a monster that is wisdom–folly, as we have found Hamlet telling Ophelia. Hamlet's own delight in this figure conjured up by him must be called merely intellectual rather than complete. But in what Hamlet says about Yorick there is the hint of a monster that could be called authority–folly, formed of a king and his attendant jester, and this is a monster in which Hamlet seems to take delight of the heart as well as delight of the mind. From what Hamlet says we know how Yorick's 'jibes', directed at assembled authority in the King's palace, and Yorick's 'gambols', his 'songs', and his 'flashes of merriment' had their own recognized power, even over authority, and 'were wont to set the table on a roar'. King Hamlet gave acceptance to this power. Thereby, we may say, the fool joined with the King in the power of the ruler's office and the King joined with the fool in the power of the jester's office.

Lear and his fool inevitably come to mind. In them Shakespeare works out dramatically a closeness possible in the union between king and attendant fool that he makes Hamlet to some extent suggest. Hamlet suggests the possibility by the affection he shows he was capable of feeling for Yorick in childhood ('Here hung those lips that I have kissed I know not how oft') and is still capable of feeling, along with mature appreciation, now that he is a prince looking to be put on as king. Lear has a marked dependence upon his 'pretty knave' and sadly misses him when he has 'not seen him this two days'; and it shows something of what the fool is capable of feeling for Lear as well as for Cordelia that after Cordelia's going into France he is reported to have much pined away' (*King Lear*, I. iv. 78–80). When Lear meets stinging but necessary jests from the fool with a warning to take heed of the whip, his words seem to have less meaning as a threat to the fool than as an intimation that he himself must be whipped by the truth. As the drama of Lear and the fool takes form their feeling one for the other proves to be part of a remarkable force. This force draws them so closely together that one tends toward being the other. The fool becomes Lear's other self, debating with him and revealing to him his predicament. And by the revelation a king knows himself as a fool. Lear's fool is 'boy' to Lear. But as early as the first scene in which the two appear, the fool gives Lear the name of boy in return: 'Dost know the difference, my boy, between a bitter fool and a sweet fool?' (I. iv. 152–3.) The answer to Lear's question then asked—'Dost thou call me a fool, boy?'— comes in varying forms of yes, over and over again, in this and following scenes. And Lear comes to call himself fool soon enough:

> O Lear, Lear, Lear!
> Beat at this gate that let thy folly in
> (I. iv. 292–3).

In the trial scene, when Lear imagines his ungrateful daughters arraigned before learned 'justicers', he makes the fool one of the judges and addresses him as 'sapient sir' (III. vi. 24). In madness he sees in the fool and in the supposedly crazed Edgar that part of himself which judges the daughters. One thing that can be said about the disappearance of the fool from the play at the end of this scene is that at the point where he gets due recognition from Lear for the sapience he has contributed to him the way is open for a complete absorption into Lear. There comes a time when he needs no longer to be a separate self of Lear.

Lear and Hamlet both have within them majesty–folly and wisdom–folly in grotesque unions of incompatible things such as we have seen imaged by Hamlet's imagination. Each has an antic part to play as well as a royal part and each turns to antic figures around him as he explores folly to find in it something more than folly. Lear has an incomparable attendant fool with whom he joins ever more closely, and he goes from majesty even into a state of crazed 'natural' foolishness in the process of gaining wisdom. Hamlet lacks an attendant fool like Lear's but has an incomparable capacity to be a prince and at the same time his own attendant fool in his search for truth.

To his Cleopatra Shakespeare has given much of a grotesqueness of majesty–folly, though almost nothing of any grotesqueness of wisdom–folly. For the making of an effective alliance with wisdom her folly is too much in and for herself. She has very little indeed of the urge to explore and appreciate folly in others that is in Hamlet and Lear. What she does in her encounter with the clownish bringer of the worm whose 'biting is immortal' comes in some part to such appreciative exploration, especially when she invites him to be most himself by her mock-innocent question, 'Will it eat me?' But by this time she is a very impatient listener. After the pertinent and impertinent rambling reply in which he makes out that 'a woman is a dish for the gods, if the devil dress her not' she tells him bluntly to go: 'Well, get thee gone; farewell.' She has tried twice before in forty lines of dialogue, just as bluntly, to be rid of him. The exploration here, then, suffers by comparison with Hamlet's fascinated probing of the clownish gravedigger. Nevertheless, it leads to the grotesque master-stroke in which Shakespeare joins the anti-elevation in the clown's words about the asp's immortal biting to the elevation in Cleopatra's words that immediately follow the clown's exit:

> Give me my robe, put on my crown. I have
> Immortal longings in me
> (*Antony and Cleopatra*, v. ii. 283–4).[1]

6

When Shakespeare makes much of the fool in plays other than *Hamlet* and *King Lear*, he does so in a group of comedies of which *As You Like It* is generally taken to be the earliest and among

[1] As A. P. Rossiter has helpfully maintained in an essay on 'Comic Relief', 'it is not eccentric to be dissatisfied with' the idea that the grotesque in Shakespearean tragedy is a means of mercifully lowering tragic tensions (*Angel with Horns, and Other Shakespeare Lectures*, London, 1961, p. 275).

which, for lack of more fitting association, *Troilus and Cressida* may be included. In these the bond between folly and not-folly is notably weaker than we have seen it in *Hamlet* and *King Lear*. One may be surprised to find it so. It might be expected to be more nearly of the same order.

Because the Jaques of *As You Like It* has in mild form some of the qualities of Hamlet, the tie that exists between him and Touchstone comes to mind at once. The melancholy of Jaques, like that of Hamlet, is caused by more than revulsion from a foulness discovered in the 'body of the infected world', since for him too there are discords within himself as well as discords between what is within and what is without. He is 'compact of jars', as the banished Duke says, and one of these comes from his double feeling toward Touchstone and toward the folly Touchstone stands for. A counterpart of this is in Hamlet's double feeling toward the grave-digging clown and toward the clown's sort of folly. In each case there is feeling for and feeling against, with the first feeling coming mostly from admiration for the *métier* of the fool or clown and the second mostly from looking down on the man himself as an 'ass' (Hamlet's term), low on the scale of humanity though strangely clever. Jaques is no prince, but he has enough of the mark of the landed gentry upon him to be accused by Rosalind of selling his lands in order to get funds for the travels by which he has purchased his melancholy. As a gentleman he cannot forget that what he readily responds to in Touchstone is contained in a man to whom by rights he should not be responding at all. The captured learning out of which Touchstone extracts foolery is to Jaques 'knowledge ill-inhabited, worse than Jove in a thatch'd house (III. iii. 10–11).

Jaques means it truly enough when he says of Touchstone and Audrey, as they join other lovers who are gathering at the end of the play like couples entering the ark before a new flood, that they are 'a pair of very strange beasts, which in all tongues are call'd fools'. But he also means it truly enough, with an irony that somehow does not kill off all of the simpler meaning, when he presents Touchstone to the Duke as 'the motley-minded gentleman that

I have so often met in the forest'. However little of the gentleman
Jaques actually sees about Touchstone, he at least hates to see him,
a man of his 'breeding', standing with Audrey to 'be married
under a bush like a beggar'. He foresees disaster for him married
to Audrey at all. At the end, after assigning other principals of the
play to happy fortunes, he turns to Touchstone with:

> And you to wrangling, for thy loving voyage
> Is but for two months victuall'd.

We remember Touchstone's ominous wish, expressed earlier,
that the gods had made Audrey 'poetical' enough to 'second' him
with the forward child Understanding. For the fool who is but
a clown, one with no forwardness in knowing, Jaques has only
aversion. In the way of fool Audrey is to him no better than the
open-mouthed William, but Touchstone he credits with a mind,
'motley' though it be. Jaques does not have the large capacity for
acceptance of folly that leads Hamlet to enjoy the performance of
even an unknowing fool.

Nor does Jaques actually show that, like Hamlet, he has the
desire and the ability to play the knowing fool himself. His talk
about being 'ambitious for a motley coat' quickly drifts into talk
about provisos after the Duke says 'Thou shalt have one' (II. vii.
43–4). The provisos have to do with his being given a fool's freedom to cleanse the foul world by speaking his mind. He does not
go beyond satire in envisioning what he would offer as a fool. He
is far from getting to any Erasmian praise of folly in the large. The
truth is that Shakespeare has given him a melancholy that is merely
sentimental and a love of clever folly that is equally sentimental.
He does not suffer from melancholy but savours it. He is amusing
enough as he does so. He is a privileged oddity in the entourage
of the Duke, kept as an attendant entertainer somewhat as a fool
would be. In other words, he already has the freedom to rail that
he says he would like to have as a fool. He does not want to pay
the cost of being looked down upon as a wearer of motley in order
to gain whatever else belongs to an attendant fool. Shakespeare
has sport with Jaques in the same spirit in which he makes Jaques

have sport with Touchstone. He finds the creation of Jaques good,
he shows him off, he says to us: 'Good my lords, like this fellow.'
But he no more supports the pretence of Jaques to qualities of
a good fool than Jaques supports the pretence of Touchstone to
qualities of a good courtier. In fact, Shakespeare is rather cruel to
him in one scene where he shows a calamitous gap in his readiness
of wit, making him deficient in what the good fool depends upon
in meeting all challengers. Jaques is most ignominiously put down
in a not too exacting wit combat with Orlando and in retreat can
manage only this weak parting shot: 'I'll tarry no longer with you.
Farewell, good Signior Love' (iii. ii. 309–10). Shakespeare is here,
of course, going about the romantic business of showing love as
comic conqueror. But we are allowed to realize that Touchstone,
competent fool that he is, could certainly not have been used as
the sufferer of defeat here in place of Jaques. So much removed is
Jaques, then, from Hamlet, who as a knower and practiser of
folly is not shaped for comic defeat, not even in casual encounter.
Hamlet's tragic defeat is all the more moving when we see him
undefeated comically.

Touchstone and Feste are brother fools and yet, as in the case
of the plays in which they appear, there is a marked difference
between them along with a marked relationship. In *As You Like It*
'winter and rough weather' are sung about (not by Touchstone)
as the only enemy, though it is not a very threatening one for
those who are living in an Arcadian summer. *Twelfth Night*, however, ends with a song (by Feste) about 'the wind and the rain',
which has it that 'the rain it raineth every day' in a world where
those who are no longer children know that

> 'Gainst knaves and thieves men shut their gate
>
> (v. i. 404–5).

In this world of *Twelfth Night* there is more than a little gate-
shutting against fools as well as knaves and thieves. Unknowing
pretentious fools suffer from it particularly. There is not ill will
enough in the world of *As You Like It* to produce anything like
what happens when Malvolio and Sir Andrew Aguecheek are

'most notoriously abused' by those who are cleverer than they. Sir Toby Belch as a leader of these abusers is a Falstaff turned strangely incapable of carrying his drink level-headedly and strangely capable of pure viciousness in disaster, as when he refuses help from Sir Andrew just because this gull of his is 'an ass-head and a coxcomb and a knave—a thin-faced knave' (v. i. 212–13). Feste is, of course, not formed to undergo heartless trickery like Malvolio and Sir Andrew, but with the tie of human feeling as weak as it is between these two grossly unknowing fools on one side and the tricksters who work upon them on the other, the tie between the admirably knowing Feste and his patrons and companions seems to be adversely affected. Feste suffers from having somewhat less than his due from those around him, as Bradley says in paying him tribute.

Bradley feels called upon to choose between Touchstone and Feste as though he might take one of them as an attendant fool for himself. The essay in which he makes his choice begins thus: 'Lear's Fool stands in a place apart—a sacred place; but, of Shakespeare's other Fools, Feste, the so-called Clown in *Twelfth Night*, has always lain nearest to my heart. He is not, perhaps, more amusing than Touchstone, to whom I bow profoundly in passing; but I love him more.'[1] If it is hard for us now to make consideration of Shakespeare's three best professional fools so much a matter of worship and love, we still do not need to deny the perception that Bradley shows as he fixes upon what he likes in Feste. He holds that Feste is much more able than Touchstone to take care of himself in the way of the world. Feste is forehanded as a beggar of money, apparently in a good thrifty spirit, and he is very discreet and knowing at handling politically the opposing forces in the household to which he is attached. We may or may not respond sympathetically to Bradley's liking for these qualities, but they exist in Feste. Bradley has further feeling for Feste as an engaging fool who, within the play, is an unloved fool, however much he is recognized as wise at playing the fool. Compassion presses

[1] A. C. Bradley, 'Feste the Jester', *A Book of Homage to Shakespeare*, ed. Israel Gollancz, Oxford, 1916, p. 164.

perhaps too hard in favour of a Feste not duly loved when Bradley
says of him, 'In important respects he is, more than Shakespeare's
other fools, superior in mind to his superiors in rank.' But the
point is well worth making that between high and low, when
Feste is the low, no very strong bond is created through appreciation of low by high. Feste is accepted as an entertaining practiser
of his profession by those who occupy high place, much as he is
by those who do not. That is all. He is thoroughly accepted, but
merely accepted. No witty young ladies choose him as companion
on a journey of pastoral discovery, and no Jaques yearns senti-
mentally for a share of his folly.

Against Thersites in *Troilus and Cressida* and Lavatch in *All's
Well that Ends Well* there is even more shutting of the gate, because they are true knaves as well as attendant fools. Yet each also
has a definite measure of acceptance by the high.

Lavatch is over and over said to be a knave, not always with the
worst implications but frequently in a way that leaves him knave
indeed. He is called foul-mouthed and calumnious knave, knave
and fool, shrewd knave, and unhappy knave. The Countess of
Rossillion, in whose service he is, joins in the chorus against him,
but spends time to draw him out in his foolery, and can be moved
to make excuses for him. She says of him to the old Lord Lafew,
'My lord that's gone made himself much sport out of him. By his
authority he remains here, which he thinks is a patent for his
sauciness; and indeed he has no pace, but runs where he will' (IV.
v. 67–71). If, after admitting that he has his good moments now
and then, we find Lavatch growing tiresome, we can accept support from Lafew. Just before the Countess apologizes for the
quality of her inherited fool, Lafew has brought one of Lavatch's
performances to an end with this dismissal: 'Go thy ways, I begin
to be aweary of thee; and I tell thee so before, because I would
not fall out with thee.' One may be tempted to think that with
Lavatch on his hands Shakespeare himself proved able to grow
aweary of the attendant fool with an established place in a royal or
noble household. If so, he was still to have a revival of interest in
that kind of fool's grotesque possibilities before casting him off,

and this would make his achievement of Lear's fool all the more remarkable.

As for Thersites, he is declared 'a privileged man' as a jester and is otherwise favoured with support by Achilles, but he is vastly different from any other attendant fool of Shakespeare's. By being what he is he contributes to a new form of the Shakespearean grotesque in a way that will be considered in my next chapter.

7

It is clear that as Shakespeare is led to write *Hamlet* he is similarly led, in a period beginning not long before and ending not long after his work upon *Hamlet*, to take the knowing figure of folly through a transformation. In this period he varies the unknowing fool and increases his grotesque validity, in a William, a Sir Andrew Aguecheek, a Malvolio, a Polonius, an Osric, an Elbow, and a Froth, but he does not alter this figure essentially. It is the perceptive maker of the jest, not the unperceptive butt of the jest, that undergoes sea-change at his hands.

Hamlet is pre-eminently a drama of human knowing and failing to know, and it includes in its dramatic field, as something by no means minor, the knowing that man gains through perceptive folly. The hero of the play practises folly, partly because he needs to protect himself by playing the fool, but even more, one must conclude, because he seeks knowledge by playing the fool. He finds the process infinitely attractive, whether he seeks to know that the King is his father's murderer, or simply to know, in the large. As his own fool, Hamlet is the most profound in the line of Shakespeare's dedicated practisers of folly that begins apparently with Touchstone and ends with Lear's fool. He too, and more than Feste orany other of these, deserves to be called 'wise enough to play the fool'.

When Shakespeare came to develop uses for the attendant fool and to make much of this figure that occurs with what has been called 'surprising rarity' in Elizabethan drama generally, he was fortunate in having Robert Armin, as a recently acquired member of his company, to play fools' parts.¹ But that Armin, however effective he was in such parts, led Shakespeare to all that he did with the attendant fool one need not suppose. Behind the Shakespearean attendant fool there is Falstaff, the jester who is attendant upon a prince and has credentials of knighthood almost as dubious as Touchstone's credentials of courtiership.

¹ The rarity of the fully developed attendant fool in Elizabethan plays apart from Shakespeare's is commented upon at length by Olive Mary Busby, *Studies in the Development of the Fool in Elizabethan Drama*, Oxford, 1923. On Armin in relation to Shakespeare see particularly: T. W. Baldwin, 'Shakespeare's Jester: The Dates of *Much Ado* and *As You Like It*', *Modern Language Notes*, xxxix (1924), p. 451; Enid Welsford, *The Fool: His Social and Literary History*, London, 1935, pp. 163 ff.; Leslie Hotson, *Shakespeare's Motley*, New York, 1952, pp. 88 ff.; and Charles S. Felver, 'Robert Armin, Shakespeare's Fool: A Biographical Essay', *Kent State University Bulletin*, xlix (1961).

V

DIABOLIC GROTESQUENESS:
THERSITES, IAGO, AND CALIBAN

1

WITH the creation of the sinister Thersites in *Troilus and Cressida* Shakespeare gives to an attendant fool a quality of diabolic malice such as he has not given before to either clown or fool. Nothing that Hamlet finds in his exploration of folly and nothing of folly that he practises prepares for this transformation of the fool in a play which is tied closely to *Hamlet* in poetic manner and may well have immediately followed it.

The grave-digging clown in *Hamlet* might in a way be called a sinister grotesque figure. He has delight in bringing any man's dust home to the earth whence it was taken. Yet he has a remarkable lack of malice. He works happily at his occupation of burying mankind but shows not the slightest ill will toward mankind. He is like the figure of Death in the later Dance of Death, in that he is a reminder that all men must die, but is as grotesquely comic as Death comes to be in sixteenth-century versions of the Dance after having been merely gruesome in earlier versions. The figure of Death begins to take on comicality in much the same way as, though at a later time than, the grotesques in manuscript illumination. The comic Death may play practical jokes on his victims in the Dance or caper with joy as he conducts them to the grave, but he expresses no more animosity toward mankind than the grave-digging clown in *Hamlet*.[1] After all, both he and this clown are free from any need to call down ill upon mankind in order to have

---

[1] For the coming of comedy into the Dance of Death see Leonard P. Kurtz, *The Dance of Death and the Macabre Spirit in European Literature*, New York, 1934, pp. 194 ff.

members of it to bury. They are satisfied to accept the unfailing succession of gifts that the common fate of mortal humanity puts into their hands. They can even do so with a certain amiability made possible by what, in the clown, is called by Horatio 'a property of easiness'.

Thersites lacks entirely the amiability of the gravedigger in *Hamlet*, which is also discoverable to a greater or lesser extent in all previous clowns and fools of Shakespeare's. This can show itself not merely as complaisance toward humanity in general but as amused tolerance or appreciation of, or even left-handedly benevolent support for, the non-grotesque high by the grotesque low. Thersites is never complaisant toward any man and has an all-inclusive ill will. But most particularly he is inimical to all that mankind has set up as worthy of high regard within its ranks and within its codes of action.

2

Thersites is an attendant fool who goes to war, and Falstaff, capable of the 'fool-born jest', is an attendant Vice who goes to war. To see what Thersites is in temper that Falstaff is not is instructive. To see what the setting of Thersites is that the setting of Falstaff is not is likewise instructive.

Troilus and Cressida turns almost as much upon the concept of honour in warfare as any of the plays in the trilogy devoted to Henry IV and Henry V. But in concern with codified high endeavour it goes beyond any play in that trilogy. It turns upon the concept of love as well as upon that of honour. For Troilus most notably, but for some other Trojans characteristically, love can become courtly love that demands full allegiance from the warrior who has faith-keeping honour.

Holding usually to a place on the margin of this drama of war and love is Thersites. He participates less than Falstaff in central action and when he keeps aloof is less in accord with it in the way of grotesquely echoing it or producing echoes within it. There is nothing in *Troilus and Cressida* that compares with the theme of thievery echoed back and forth between Falstaffian grotesque and royal non-grotesque. The reason is simply that Thersites by nature seeks to avoid action. He tends to reject possible action offered to him or, better still, to keep action from taking on possibility for him. We do not see anything of Thersites as grotesquely encountering a challenge of love. He keeps that challenge from being made by not exposing himself to a Doll Tearsheet who might be a marginal counterpart of Helen or Cressida. But we do see Thersites encountering two challenges to combat on the battlefield, where, like Falstaff, he exposes himself to the possibility of action at the centre of things. There he is just as surely a figure of anti-honour as Falstaff. Yet there is a difference between them that goes deep.

The difference is that Falstaff, when challenged by Douglas to participate in combat, is grotesque in acceptance and performance, whereas Thersites, when similarly challenged, first by Hector and then by Margarelon, is grotesque merely in rejection. Falstaff is finely endowed with plausible presumption, which perhaps should be called the supreme grotesque gift. Thersites is not endowed with this at all. When acting in the way of extreme dishonour Falstaff is able to win honour—for a time and in some eyes—as he pretends death to end the combat with Douglas, rises to stab the dead Hotspur, and bears off Hotspur's corpse to justify a reward from the Prince. Thersites, however, when acting in the way of extreme dishonour can only declare brazenly that he does so. Asked by Hector whether he is 'Hector's match' as a man 'of blood and honour', he is glad to be believed as he says he is nothing but 'a very filthy rogue' (v. iv. 28–31). Confronted on the field by Margarelon, who announces himself as 'a bastard son of Priam's', he gets himself passed by as a coward not worth fighting with. He turns away the challenge with words that are utterly self-derogatory by any non-grotesque standard: 'I am a bastard too; I love bastards. I am bastard begot, bastard instructed, bastard in mind, bastard in valour, in everything illegitimate' (v. vii. 16–19).

In these actions Thersites is facing down not merely threats to his life but also threats to his inner man and its convictions. In the completeness of his illegitimacy and lowness he is defying utterly the legitimate high. He is refusing to let it bring him to terms with its code of honour even when it descends to the trickery of confronting him with royal illegitimacy that will ironically uphold the code and tempt him to a combat of bastard against bastard under the code's authority.

By comparison with Falstaff, Thersites may appear to have the moral grandeur of an independent integrity. He may seem to be refusing laudably to join a way of life in which honour can be made an object of worship and can then be basely violated in many ways before it is climactically outraged by an Achilles, who will not risk man-to-man combat with Hector but has him assassinated by his Myrmidons. In *Troilus and Cressida* Shakespeare is very certainly not devoting himself to the Trojan story in the fully traditional epic spirit. The play is filled with checkmatings of high endeavour and of its supporting idealism, both in war and love, and these are found in the poetic expression as well as in the action. They cause argument among critics as to whether the drama is a wryly tragical presentation of failure in high endeavour or a satirical presentation of falseness in it. For some the running comment of Thersites upon the action and upon those who take part in it seems to be a chorus of condemnation that is comically exaggerated but is nevertheless indicative of a general direction in the drama.

But to give such weight to Thersites as a maker of choral comment is to distort both him and the drama. In the design of *Troilus and Cressida* there are many ironies, and Thersites is one of them. What is most ironic about him is that he practises honesty on the battlefield but does not do so because he is in any way virtuously opposed to dishonesty as a human failing. On the contrary he delights in all human failings, his own or anyone else's, and delights particularly in all things within the realms of love and war that he can find to be shortcomings. It must be remarked that, as Shakespeare has presented the opponents in the war, Thersites can discover such things among his fellowship of Greeks more easily than among the Trojans. But it must also be remarked that Thersites is simply not looking for other things among either Trojans

or Greeks, and thus in his limitations fails as a chorus. To those
around him in the play he is repellent, though intriguingly so.
He is accepted ambivalently by his patron Achilles, for whom he
has the acknowledged attraction of serving as an aid to digestion at
dinner by taking the place of piquantly decayed cheese. But Thersites pays them all back. He takes them to be as repellent as they
take him to be and at the same time as intriguing in the way of
tasty corruption.

   With the change in the Shakespearean grotesque figure that
comes with Thersites, there is a change in the grotesque use of
animal imagery. Typically it becomes name-calling and registers
detestation of the one to whom it is applied, whether it is used by
Thersites against another or by another against him. It may have
some particular aptness, as when Thersites, making the jest on the
cuckold's horns of Menelaus which is recurrent in the play, calls
him a 'bull, the primitive statue and oblique memorial of cuckolds'.
But then again the loathing of Thersites for Menelaus may produce in his imagination a random lot of animal unattractiveness for
purposes of comparison. He may ask himself 'to what form but
that he is should wit larded with malice, and malice forced with
wit, turn him to?' In part he may answer: 'To be a dog, a mule, a
cat, a fitchook, a toad, a lizard, an owl, a puttock, or a herring
without a roe, I would not care. But to be Menelaus! I would
conspire against destiny. Ask me not what I would be if I were not
Thersites, for I care not to be the louse of a lazar, so I were not
Menelaus' (v. i. 60–72). Here malice does not lard wit so much as
it renders wit volubly indiscriminate. The assignment of animality
to Thersites in exchange for his own name-calling can aptly
enough make him a 'porpentine' in his prickliness and a 'dog' or
'dam'ed cur' or 'bitch-wolf's son' in his snappishness. But when,
for example, Ajax calls him a 'vile owl', there seems again to be
indiscriminate vituperation. Animal imagery which helps to present the figure of Thersites, used either by him about others or by
others about him, is not to be compared for wealth of grotesque
significance with that which helps similarly to present the figure
of Falstaff.

One reason is that Thersites has no such endowment of monstrosity as Falstaff's. He is, of course, as monstrous in the largeness of his spleen and its ill will as Falstaff is in the largeness of his belly and its appetite. But to such simple monstrosity he adds very little of a monstrosity of incongruities. For one thing, what is unappealingly animal in him never shows itself joined to something appealingly animal. The bovine in Falstaff in its unappealing form is joined with a form that is 'sweet beef', but the canine in Thersites has no form better than 'damn'd cur'. So dominant is the currishness in Thersites that it gives him a cur's eye to find kindred around him: 'that same dog-fox Ulysses', 'that mongrel cur Ajax', and 'that dog of as bad a kind, Achilles' (v. iv. 12–15). Here once more malice works against wit. One recognizes that in Thersites wit does join itself incongruously with animality, but that in him neither wit nor animality comes near to having Falstaffian copiousness. The two together are much less than Falstaffian in power to form dramatic opposition between them.

Most striking is the total absence in Thersites of a doubleness comparable with that which makes Falstaff in one way a proper champion of the low and in another way an openhearted supporter of the high. Falstaff supports the high as an existent order, whatever reservations he has about following its codes himself. He does so because he realizes that he can best follow his grotesque nature by attaching himself to the non-grotesque and because he finds true gratification as one of the low in being second father to a scion of the high. Even before the creation of Falstaff, as we have seen, it is characteristic of the Shakespearean grotesque figure to show good will in some form for the high and at times lend it support. But Thersites is so far from having any such goodwill that he can call down a curse from Olympus upon Ajax and Achilles, the chief Greek performers in arms, and for good measure then cry: 'After this, the vengeance on the whole camp! or rather the Neapolitan bone-ache! for that methinks is the curse dependent on those that war for a placket. I have said my prayers; and devil Envy say "Amen!" ' Before his calling for a devil's Amen to his prayers the diabolic malice of Thersites has led him to swear, ' 'Sfoot, I'll learn to conjure and raise devils but I'll see some issue of my spiteful execrations' (II. iii. 6–25).

Falstaff is given the name of Vice by Prince Hal and is properly recognized as an Elizabethan version of the medieval Vice by those who now discuss him, but in one important respect he is lacking as a Vice as Thersites is not. He is, as I have said, not one who wants others to suffer so that he may enjoy their suffering, though he is quite willing to have them suffer that he may live more fully a life of ease. Thersites, on the other hand, is very much for having others suffer just so he may enjoy their suffering. It is not for nothing that he calls upon the devil Envy to support his supplication to Olympus for a curse upon the Greek camp. He is on that devil's side, as Falstaff is not. His calling upon a devil after praying to Olympian gods is a waggish grotesque anachronism. It is somewhat like the anachronism of the fool in *King Lear* which is perpetrated when that fool, a pagan, offers a prophecy in which he mentions the burning of heretics and the building of churches as going on about him in an obviously Christian age and then announces: 'This prophecy Merlin shall make, for I live before his time' (III. ii. 5–6). Making experience of time almost as monstrous as Lear's fool makes it, Thersites, a pagan, shows Italian Renaissance knowledge of the syphilitic bone-ache and is a medieval Vice as a fool upon the Elizabethan stage.

But though as a Vice Thersites is all he should be in evil-willing and also in calling for infernal support, he is not all he should be in evil-doing. He is not a true tempter of those around him. He does not in devious ways get them to fight each other. He does not even trick them in minor ways. By choice he simply watches on the edge of action and gloats over all human failings that he observes. It must be granted that with things as they are around him, particularly among the Greeks, he does not greatly need to create or cultivate failings in those he watches. In the general company of evil he is, like any Vice, very plainly of a low order, however much he can be credited with diabolism. But even in the company of Vices he is so low in predatory instincts that he is only a jackal.

3

Thersites is more sinister as an enemy of love than as an enemy of honour, even though he is shown twice in scornful rejection of a challenge of honour on the battlefield and not shown at all in rejection of a challenge of love. As a diabolic enemy of love he looks forward toward the most sinister of all among Shakespearean grotesque figures. He looks toward Iago. No matter how far apart Thersites and Iago may be found to be in some respects, they come together closely in one respect. Toward love both are most devotedly inimical. An approach to Iago by way of Thersites is now my concern.

Thersites is the passive, though ardent, enemy of an order of human mating that has set fleshly desire within a cultural structure and made marriage and courtly love parts of the whole. Courtly love may be taken under one aspect as antagonistic to marriage. Yet under another aspect it may be taken as firmly allied to marriage. Codes that give form to it and to marriage provide for both a foundation in faith-keeping. And violation of the faith-keeping that is enjoined for both makes a central theme in *Troilus and Cressida*. Troilus the courtly lover can speak of faith-keeping in marriage as most highly honourable and rightly to be followed. He can do so while he is suing for Cressida without any intention whatever of entering into marriage with her. But by the end of the play, after faithfulness in Troilus and unfaithfulness in Cressida have run their courses entirely outside marriage, it is plain that Troilus has put himself with all honesty into the eloquent words he has spoken about marriage:

> I take to-day a wife, and my election
> Is led on in the conduct of my will,
> My will enkindled by mine eyes and ears,
> Two traded pilots 'twixt the dangerous shores
> Of will and judgment. How may I avoid,
> Although my will distaste what it elected,
> The wife I chose? There can be no evasion
> To blench from this and to stand firm by honour
>
> (II. ii. 61-8).

Troilus here has spoken of marriage for himself hypothetically, in order to support an argument that to maintain honour the Trojans must carry on the war with the Greeks no matter what reasons have been found for not doing so. They must go on with the war because at its beginning they solemnly gave themselves to it as to a just cause and they must now keep faith with that cause. They are, so to speak, married to it. Yet though the words have been spoken by a Troilus who was an all-or-nothing adherent of faith-keeping in warfare, they have proved later to be entirely suitable for a Troilus no less intense as an adherent of faith-keeping in courtly love. To think it one of the many ironies in the play that Troilus should pay tribute to marriage as he does is to see him merely in latter-day terms as 'having an affair' with Cressida.

Thersites takes delight in all shortcomings that make for divisiveness in humanity and he is thus inimical to love in its largest sense. But he takes a very particular delight in human failure to live up to a culturally enjoined faith-keeping for sexual union. He would have salaciousness thrive, not for its capacity to bring about sexual union but for its capacity to bring about sexual promiscuity and thus to break sexual union once it is formed, especially any union formed on a basis of faith-keeping. If faithlessness in love produces combat, his delight is enhanced. Throughout the play he is full of derision for the war that has been precipitated by Helen's faithlessness in marriage and her husband's following of a code of honour in taking the matter to the battlefield. Yet he is also full of satisfaction that the war exists. He avidly follows the struggle and is so far from being a moral satirist opposing warfare that he can pray to have 'war and lechery confound all'.

When the theme of cuckold and whore that begins with Helen's faithlessness in marriage comes to be repeated with Cressida's faithlessness in courtly love and her bringing of Troilus to be the sworn enemy of Diomed, the cup of Thersites is full. The 'devil Luxury', at the call of the 'devil Envy', has had his way and the injunction 'fry, lechery, fry!' has had effect. As Thersites capers around the combatants on the battlefield at the end of the play he characteristically makes heroic cuckolds take on grotesquely ignoble animal forms. Troilus fighting Diomed for a Cressida who is a dissembling luxurious drab is a young Trojan ass, and Menelaus fighting Paris for a Helen who is the acme of whorish falseness is a bull baited by a dog.

As for the lust of the flesh that man shares with animals, this is seen by Thersites as never to be taken lightly, even in bawdy jesting. It means too much to him for that. Its existence, to be earnestly gloated over, brings too much satisfaction to him. Thersites is merely an obsessed observer of lechery and yet he has much more weight dramatically as a supporter of the cause of lechery than the bawd Pompey in *Measure for Measure*, who actively promotes what the Duke in that play calls the 'abominable and beastly touches' of human mating. For Pompey follows bawdry with a certain amused philosophical detachment and finally is prevailed upon to be false to his calling.

One is reminded that the earlier Shakespearean grotesque can set itself against the love that soars but does so in a way not at all like the sinister way of Thersites. It does so notably in *Romeo and Juliet*. The Nurse in that play is one of the company of the unknowing grotesque, like the Hostess of the Boar's Head. She realizes little of what she does on occasions when she hinders the soaring of love. She can even think she encourages it. Of course, when Mercutio turns grotesque he is knowingly so and is well aware of what he does as he puts a check upon love. But both he and she check love and yet serve its cause as they do so. Each contributes to the consciousness in soaring love that without making common cause with the lust of the flesh it will not have an abiding place in sexual union. And both have a bawdy goodwill toward the love they work upon and toward the two who are entering upon its experience. Mercutio is without malice and even shows a grotesque amiability when he will have it that love is a drivelling fool, 'a great natural that runs lolling up and down to hide his bauble in a hole' (II. iv. 96–7). He may be called an enemy of love only if he is called a friendly enemy. But where love is concerned Thersites (to take a lead from his calling of Patroclus 'a fool positive') is clearly enough an enemy positive.

4

To positiveness of enmity toward love Iago adds effectiveness that is totally lacking in Thersites. The quality he thus acquires as a willer and doer of evil and a shaper of events in *Othello* has been much argued about since Coleridge found in him 'the motive-hunting of motiveless malignity'.[1] Whether Iago may be called motiveless and thus not realistically human in his intense malignity has become almost as much an issue as whether Falstaff may be called a coward in his intense desire to stay alive.

Iago takes pains to have himself recognized as a master crafts-man who works evil in no ordinary way. Characteristically he does not say at the beginning in the melodramatically simple manner of Richard III that he is determined to follow an evil course. He challenges us to show that he does evil even as he demonstrates that he does it. In effect he boasts himself to be one who can take us into his confidence and expose his iniquity but can yet successfully defy us to incriminate him. The boast is made as he plots to have Desdemona intercede with Othello for the cashiered Cassio. Desdemona, he says, is of 'so blessed a disposition she holds it a vice in her goodness not to do more than she is requested'. Iago is not one to belittle goodness. He is one to give it full recognition and encouragement—for his own purposes. By furthering the cause of goodness, a goodness of action in Des-demona and a goodness of hope in Cassio, he will achieve some-thing opposite to what these two look for. But who can maintain that what is thus achieved, coming as it does through good, is to be called evil?

Here we find a problem of evil in relation to good that is ever present in the Christian tradition. How is it that evil can issue from good and likewise good from evil? The second part of this prob-lem takes its best-known concrete form in the Paradox of the Fortunate Fall, which comes in Milton's hands to be the climax of justification for the ways of God to man in *Paradise Lost*. The

[1] *Coleridge's Shakespearean Criticism*, ed. T. M. Raysor, Cambridge, Massa-chusetts, 1930, i. 49.

whole of the problem Friar Laurence states succinctly in *Romeo and Juliet*:

> Virtue itself turns vice, being misapplied,
> And vice sometime's by action dignified
>
> (II. iii. 21–2).

For his own benefit Iago explores the problem at some length in a soliloquy after he has urged Cassio to importune Desdemona for help. His ability at the opening of this soliloquy to see a bringing of good out of his own evil is formidable:

> And what's he then that says I play the villain,
> When this advice is free I give and honest,
> Probal to thinking, and indeed the course
> To win the Moor again? For 'tis most easy
> Th' inclining Desdemona to subdue
> In any honest suit. . . .
>   . . . How am I then a villain
> To counsel Cassio to this parallel course,
> Directly to his good?
>
> (II. iii. 342–56.)

In these lines he turns his own inclination into one as 'honest' as Desdemona's, thus making a contribution to the structure of irony built upon repeated use of the word 'honest' in the play. At the conclusion of his soliloquy he looks forward to a bringing of evil at its blackest out of Desdemona's goodness:

> So will I turn her virtue into pitch,
> And out of her own goodness make the net
> That shall enmesh them all.

Iago stands out among Shakespeare's nefarious schemers as having the largest share of an inheritance from the medieval Vice. Richard III is made to acknowledge a part of his own share when he says in an aside:

> Thus, like the formal Vice, Iniquity,
> I moralize two meanings in one word
>
> (*Richard III*, III. i. 82–3).

Richard, who characterizes himself in this way, and Falstaff, who gets to be called 'that reverend Vice, that grey Iniquity', thus are revealed to have something in common from a form of the Vice that merited the name Iniquity. Falstaff, whom probably no one would think of ranking among Shakespeare's villains for his lack of probity, has somewhat more of the Vice than the villain Richard. But Iago, whom probably no one would think of calling Falstaffian, has much more of the Vice than Falstaff. The explanation lies in that which most essentially makes the Vice what he is as distinguished from the dramatic villain.

The Vice of dramatic tradition has a man's shape but schemes and works against mankind viciously and is at heart not a man. As a figure of depravity in man he is incompletely man. He tempts and corrupts and is moved by joy taken in his clever viciousness. He is not moved, except in pretence, by ambition to rise among men and thus to profit in the way of the world by his ill deeds.

The usual Shakespearean villain, by contrast, is consumingly ambitious. He is a clever schemer doing harm to others with the basic purpose of advancing himself in the world, though often he gets much enjoyment from his viciousness. The less delight he takes in his viciousness the less he is like the Vice. The less like the Vice he is, the more human he is. Claudius in *Hamlet* is to the hero of the play a 'bloody, bawdy, villain', who has by murder appropriated a crown and a queen. In his nefariousness he is also to the hero 'a Vice of kings'. But to us he can appear pitifully human as he takes so little delight in the evil he has done that he attempts repentant prayer and struggles against himself in a way by no means Vice-like. Cassius plays villain in *Julius Caesar*. He tempts and corrupts Brutus in Vice-like fashion, but his ambition is not Vice-like, and when he participates in the catastrophe that his scheming has helped to bring about, he is completely human.

Richard III is the ambitiousvillain in fullest development, made into a tragic hero. As he seizes and attempts to hold a kingship he is moved by delight in evil-doing almost as much as by ambition, but not so much as to be kept from eventually having an attack of conscience. This is something that the Vice in full form can only pretend to have. (It should be said in passing that Macbeth is a tragic hero who rises to kingship by vicious actions but falls so far short of having any joy in them and suffers such constant agony from conscience that he is not to be put in the company of Richard or of Shakespearean villains generally.) Aaron in *Titus Andronicus* is a villain of Richard's stripe, though a lesser and more gaudily melodramatic one. He strives to 'mount aloft' with his 'imperial mistress' but achieves less than Richard and is altogether simple-minded in his cruelty, as Richard is certainly not. The satisfaction he gains from his ill deeds is to be measured in the topsy-turvy repentance of his last words:

> If one good deed in all my life I did,
> I do repent it from my very soul
>
> (v. iii. 189–90).

Yet Aaron, in the fierce love he has for his bastard son, also has his touch of humanity. And Edmund in *King Lear*, who is more subtly Ricardian in his ambitious villainy, shows humanity by turning finally to the orthodox repentance that Aaron travesties. He tries to do 'some good' before he dies by cancelling his writ on the lives of Lear and Cordelia.

A very unusual Shakespearean villain is Don John in *Much Ado about Nothing*. He receives little dramatic development and seems to have been created perfunctorily for a comic plot where temporary tribulation provided by villainy was thought to be called for. But minor creation though he is, he points toward the major creation that is Iago. He claims a motive for malignity somewhat like the one claimed by Iago. Iago declares himself disaffected because the theoretician Cassio, instead of himself, has been made Othello's lieutenant. Don John declares himself disaffected because 'the most exquisite Claudio', instead of himself, has been made 'the right hand' in military actions of his brother Don Pedro. 'That young start-up', Don John says, 'hath all the glory of my overthrow' (I. ii. 68–9). The result of disaffection in each instance is a plot to destroy love between a man and a woman by a false demonstration of unfaithfulness in the woman. Where Iago's work of deception is extended and masterful, Don John's, or rather that which he approves for his follower Borachio, is brief and to a viewer of the play can be unimpressive. But in the play it serves. It convinces Claudio that his Hero is 'every man's Hero'.[1]

For Don John, then, as well as for Iago, if each is to be believed, the foundation of disaffection is loss of military preferment. But for each there is early evidence of delight in the discovery of what Don John calls 'a model to build mischief on'. The delight is such that possibility for mischief-making begins quickly to seem the important thing, rather than any check offered to ambition. It turns out that in neither Don John nor Iago is there an ambition so pressing that it works for advancement unremittingly. After making statements at first about thwarted ambition both are strangely unconcerned about ways in which plotting can raise them to higher position. What they devotedly plot and execute is harm for those they have justified themselves in hating and for others drawn into their field of action. As soon as Iago gets well started with his plotting he proffers to himself the extra excuse that he suspects he has been cuckolded by Othello and (as an after-thought) that he also fears Cassio with his wife. There is nothing whatever presented dramatically to provide basis for the suspicion and the fear upon which he thus soliloquizes.

Don John is called by Borachio 'the devil my master' and Iago is called by Othello 'that demi-devil'. Illogically the expression 'demi-devil' as Othello uses it means more in the way of devil than the unqualified word 'devil' as Borachio uses it. By calling Don John a devil Borachio, of course, means only that his master is an outstanding villain who is confirmed in his evil qualities, a villain worse than he, Borachio, is—as in the end proves to be the case when Borachio repents and Don John does not. Borachio speaks thus of Don John with casualness and grim pleasantry. But Othello,

[1] The part played by Aaron, Richard III, Don John, and Iago as artists in evil who work against 'the affections, duties, and pieties which create the order and harmony of human society', or, in short, against 'unity and love', is admirably characterized by Bernard Spivack, *Shakespeare and the Allegory of Evil: The History of a Metaphor in Relation to His Major Villains*, New York, 1958, pp. 43 ff.

speaking to the wronged Cassio, calls Iago a demi-devil in a spirit utterly different:

> Will you, I pray, demand that demi-devil
> Why he hath thus ensnar'd my soul and body?
>
> (v. ii. 301–2.)

In this speech there is agonized but judicious assessment of Iago's evil action as being not half-devilish but devilish.

Don John and Borachio do to Hero some small part of the harm that Iago does to Desdemona, but they accomplish nothing against Claudio and Don Pedro such as Iago accomplishes against Othello and Cassio. As one comes at the end of Othello's tragedy to his words about devilish ensnarement of his soul and body one is confirmed in a feeling that throughout the play there is a poetic making of Iago into an evil figure of much deeper dye than Don John. This is done by suggestive touch after suggestive touch. Many touches are contributed by Iago himself.

After he has found the motive-hunting of motivelessness malignity in Iago, Coleridge exclaims of him: 'A being next to devil, only not quite devil—and this Shakespeare has attempted—executed—without disgust, without scandal!'[1] Here Coleridge is in good form. It is indeed a Shakespeare working apparently without disgust and with complete absorption in keeping proportion dramatically who makes Iago hold himself up to view as being more than man in evil power while bearing the natural shape of man. In Iago a Vice who plays the diabolic role of tempter and ensnarer dominates the ambitious villain. He is in large part the conventional Vice that allies himself with infernal snarers of mankind. But he has more of evil genius than the Vice of old.

5

To evil genius Iago adds evil devotion, and thus he becomes worthy to be called one of Satan's saints. In his commitment to evil he is more than willing to use the world and the flesh as corrupters of man, but he feels scorn for them as being powers that

---

[1] Op. cit., i. 49.

man would never be mastered by were it not for the depth of human folly. His respect is only for the third and greatest of the powers that are the enemies of man, the devil. He may even be called unorthodoxly ascetic in his contemning of the flesh as he gives himself to worship of the infernal and to communion with it.

The way Iago as Vice meets Roderigo's threat at the end of the first act to drown himself because of hopeless desire for Desdemona is different indeed from any earlier Vice's dealing with fleshly desire in a figure of mankind. Iago makes no suggestion that a little diversion in the way of wenching in a tavern is what is needed. He preaches masterful self-control to Roderigo that will lead the better to enjoyment of Desdemona eventually—without any mewling and puling of love. The scorn of Iago for 'the blood and baseness of our natures', and his urging of the need 'to cool our raging motions, our carnal stings, our unbitted lusts', might be approved by an early Christian desert father in the Thebaid of Egypt. That is, Iago might obtain such approval if the drift of what he says about domination of bodily lusts were not at once apparent. He would dominate these lusts simply because there is for him a greater lust to put in their place. This is the lust to know 'how to love himself' by not subjecting himself to anything but self. In that lust he aspires toward a Satanic spirituality.

Inevitably as he preaches his doctrine of self-love to Roderigo Iago reveals in all its fullness his rejection of any love whatever that goes out to another. Fond love between the sexes is as much to be mastered as the most raging motions of carnal lust, 'whereof', he says, 'I take this that you call love to be a sect or scion'. Roderigo answers (though he is not exactly a noble defender of love): 'It cannot be.' Insists Iago: 'It is merely a lust of the blood and a permission of the will.' Plainly enough love that creates the bond of friendship is for Iago something also to be mastered, since it is as much a threat to self-love as love that goes out to someone sexually desired. There is dramatic irony, with Roderigo as a gullible non-perceiver, in Iago's discoursing to him of self-love and yet keeping him a believer in his avowal of love for him. This builds toward the greater dramatic irony, with Othello as a nobly blind non-perceiver, in an interchange between Othello and Iago which comes just before Othello is brought to the conviction that Desdemona is guilty. Othello begins a speech with these lines:

> If thou dost slander her and torture me,
> Never pray more; abandon all remorse.

The self-loving Iago, as incapable of remorse and repentant prayer as he is of friendship, answers with a speech ending thus:

> Take note, take note, O world,
> To be direct and honest is not safe.
> I thank you for this profit; and from hence
> I'll love no friend, sith love breeds such offence
> (III. iii. 377–80).

Iago's iniquity as a Vice is that of the unregenerate natural in man which has grown proud and pretentious after acquiring cleverness. Characteristically it scorns the natural in man which is uncleverly and simply animal. Looking down upon love between man and woman as being never anything more than a lust of the blood, Iago fittingly enough takes it to be a weak yielding of man's precious self to enslavement by an animal instinct which should itself be the sufferer of enslavement, for man's greater pleasure.

In the images by which Iago expresses his contempt for such yielding there is striking animal grotesquery. To Roderigo's threat of suicide one reply of Iago's is this: 'Ere I would drown myself for the love of a guinea hen, I would change my humanity with a baboon.' Another reply is this: 'Drown thyself? Drown cats and blind puppies.' That is to say, a man ready to drown himself for love had better surrender his manhood and become an ape, the well-known grotesque figure of animality that presumptuously tries to be man and fails ridiculously; and a man who brings himself to drowning for love should feel shame to come to a death fit for an unwanted cat or a superfluous new-born puppy with its blind weakness.

Significantly the love of Othello and Desdemona is presented by Iago at the very beginning of the play in animal terms, even in barnyard animal terms. The father of the bride, roused from sleep on the wedding night, learns from Iago that mating is in progress between Othello, the old black ram, and Desdemona, the white ewe. Or, to change the picture, Othello, the Barbary horse, is beginning to father progeny that will neigh to their grandsire Brabantio. Or, in the even more grotesque terms of a monstrous figure used by Rabelais in a very different spirit, what goes on is a making of 'the beast with two backs'.[1] In all this Iago puts bawdy bitterness into grotesque jesting. It is far removed from the bawdy delight with which Mercutio gives a jester's recognition to the power of love by his conjuring of the strayed Romeo.

The corruption of Othello that Iago achieves makes Othello appropriate Iago's manner of seeing love as animality. When Othello is 'eaten up with passion' because of torturing uncertainty and demands absolute proof that Desdemona is unfaithful, Iago replies that of course satisfaction must be had only with 'imputation and strong circumstances'. There will never be opportunity to see Cassio and Desdemona in the very act of cuckolding him:

> It is impossible you should see this,
> Were they as prime as goats, as hot as monkeys,
> As salt as wolves in pride, and fools as gross
> As ignorance made drunk
>
> (III. iii. 402–5).

After Othello is convinced by what to him is the strong circumstance of the lost handkerchief, the picture of Desdemona and Cassio as being prime as goats and hot as monkeys remains with him. It rises before his eyes when he receives a summons to leave Cyprus, learns that Cassio is deputed to have his place there, and hears Desdemona greet the news joyfully, with implication that Cassio well deserves such restoration to favour: 'By my troth, I am glad on't.' He shocks all present, except Iago, by striking Desdemona, ordering her out of his presence, and then leaving the scene himself with an exclamation that can have meaning only for Iago—and for us: 'Goats and monkeys!' (IV. i. 247–74.)

Othello tortures himself even by adding to the repulsiveness

---

[1] The phrase is in *Pantagruel*, I. iii.

that he finds in Iago's vision of animality in love. He does so in the scene where he accuses Desdemona of falsity after he has commanded Emilia to 'leave procreants alone' and perform some of her function as 'simple bawd' by standing guard outside the door. The only procreation resulting is that of animal imagery by which he overwhelms both himself and Desdemona. He cries out to her:

> But there where I have garner'd up my heart,
> Where either I must live or bear no life,
> The fountain from the which my current runs
> Or else dries up—to be discarded thence,
> Or keep it as a cistern for foul toads
> To knot and gender in—turn thy complexion there,
> Patience, thou young and rose-lipp'd cherubin!
> Ay, there look grim as hell!

After this speech, with its knotting and gendering of concepts that finally produce a knotting and gendering of toads in a cistern, Desdemona can only say in bewildered simplicity:

> I hope my noble lord esteems me honest.

Othello replies with an image that adds further repulsiveness to animal gendering by having it thrive upon death and decay:

> O, ay! as summer flies are in the shambles,
> That quicken even with blowing (IV. ii. 66–7).

At this point, where Othello's love is converted into extreme repulsion, the most purely evil of Iago's designs has been carried out. Here, even before the bringing of death to the lovers, there is triumph for Iago in what he has set himself to do after he has looked on at the reunion of Othello and Desdemona in Cyprus, realized the concord in their love, and heard Othello say:

> I cannot speak enough of this content;
> It stops me here; it is too much of joy.

His response to this elevation of spirit in love has been a promise to himself in an aside:

> O, you are well tun'd now!
> But I'll set down the pegs that make this music.
> As honest as I am   (II. i. 201–3).

It is a response that has made him far more than merely a seeker for revenge through destruction of Othello's love for Desdemona. It has made him a devilish enemy of love itself, with an especial hatred for love's innerness, its music.

6

Iago as a Vice has the Vice's grotesque presumption, and never so much as when he pretends to be more than Vice in the army of evil. What Shakespeare would have made of a Mephistopheles if he had chosen to show one we do not know. We do know, however, that when Iago takes on the quality of a devil he is a very different worker in evil from Marlowe's Mephistopheles. He looks toward Goethe's Mephistopheles in ways that Marlowe's does not. He adds nonchalant diabolic humour to a Vice's elfin humour.

It is recognized that in *Othello* much of dramatic importance is said that rests upon concepts of hell and devils.[1] There could, I think, be increased recognition of significance in what Iago himself says as part of this.

In the first scene of the play, as Brabantio responds with angry incredulity when Iago and Roderigo tell him that his daughter has absconded and that he should take steps to recover her, Iago says: 'Zounds, sir, you are one of those that will not serve God if the devil bid you.' It is possible to take this speech as simply an apt way of saying that Brabantio is perverse in not accepting good advice from what he thinks to be a bad quarter. But in the light of matter that follows in the play Iago should, I think, be taken here as saying more. He should be taken as slyly calling himself a devil and implying, for his own satisfaction, that he has true

---

[1] A wide variety of comment on this subject appears in: Maud Bodkin, *Archetypal Patterns in Poetry: Psychological Studies of Imagination*, London, 1934, pp. 220 ff.; E. E. Stoll, *Shakespeare and Other Masters*, Cambridge, Massachusetts, 1940, pp. 233–4; S. L. Bethell, 'The Diabolic Images in *Othello*', *Shakespeare Survey*, v, ed. Allardyce Nicoll, Cambridge, 1952, pp. 62–80; Bernard Spivack, *Shakespeare and the Allegory of Evil*, New York, 1958, pp. 52 ff.; Marvin Rosenberg, *The Masks of Othello: The Search for the Identity of Othello, Iago, and Desdemona by Three Centuries of Actors and Critics*, Berkeley and Los Angeles, 1961, pp. 170–1; Leah Scragg, 'Iago—Vice or Devil?', *Shakespeare Survey*, xxi, ed. Kenneth Muir, Cambridge, 1968, pp. 53–65.

diabolic subtlety. It is subtlety by which he can help Brabantio
to perform an eminently good act and can at the same time draw
evil from its goodness for his own purposes. (By the same sublety
he later gets Desdemona to do good for Cassio in a way that produces usable evil.) Soon afterward in the first scene he says something that has a certain strangeness, unless it is accepted as part of
an assumption by him of diabolic quality. Speaking to Roderigo
he says of Othello:

> Though I do hate him as I hate hell pains,
> Yet, for necessity of present life,
> I must show out a flag and sign of love,
> Which is indeed but sign
>
> (I. i. 155–8).

The hating of hell pains seems here to come from one who knows
them as, and does not merely fear them to be, his portion. The
phrase 'for necessity of present life' is markedly ambiguous. In its
context one of its implications can be that the hater of hell pains
dwells in hell and is at present on a mission in this world.

There can be no doubt, I think, that Iago is made by Shakespeare to show pleasure in offering a picture of himself, to himself
at least, as being joined with hell. But joined just how, we are led
to ask? When he seeks to reassure Roderigo that Desdemona will
yield to him, he says: 'If sanctimony and a frail vow betwixt an
erring barbarian and a supersubtle Venetian be not too hard for
my wits and all the tribe of hell, thou shalt enjoy her.' He can
mean merely that the tribe of hell will naturally appreciate a plot
such as he will devise and that its members will seize the chance,
of their own accord, to help the plot succeed with a power greater
than his own. But as a lover and confident admirer of himself he
can mean something very different. He can mean that the tribe of
hell is subject to being summoned into action by him after his wit
has skilfully planned a campaign of evil. He can thus be implying
that he has high standing in the realm of evil.

And he can be implying the same thing in a soliloquy that comes
immediately after his attempt to reassure Roderigo. He turns there

to the making of his plot to 'abuse Othello's ear' with the suggestion that Cassio is too familiar with Desdemona. He concludes triumphantly:

> I have't! It is engend'red! Hell and night
> Must bring this monstrous birth to the world's light
>
> (I. iii. 409–10).

The images here constitute self-flattery. The extraordinary evil that is to be born has been created by Iago as its father. Hellish gestation and midwifery are to be provided for it as a matter of course.

Thus when Iago takes on the part of the Vice, he is made to be presumptuous in suggesting that he is not a Vice but a devil, and one perhaps of no low degree—a member of the tribe of hell who can summon aid from 'all the tribe'. But he is also made to be frustratingly disingenuous in a way characteristic of the Vice. He will not let himself be pinned down to claiming that he is a devil. Following good Vice tradition he plays fast and loose in what he tells about himself, to a theatre audience as well as to those he deals with in the play. He is an Ambidexter in supersubtle Venetian form.

When we come to the soliloquy that follows his persuading of the disgraced Cassio to importune Desdemona for intercession with Othello, we find Iago giving consideration to the amount of diabolic quality that he has taken on. He recognizes that if he were in all truth one of the tribe of hell, he would be concerned with capturing souls of men. As he muses upon ways in which he will enmesh his victims by having Desdemona unwittingly 'undo her credit with the Moor', he entertains the thought that Othello has a soul and that it could be captured in the right devilish fashion through perverse use of 'th' inclining Desdemona'. Because Othello's 'soul is so enfetter'd to her love', she would be able

> To win the Moor—were't to renounce his baptism—
> All seals and symbols of redeemed sin
>
> (II. iii. 349–50).

But this is no more than a passing thought. It is not the destiny of Othello's soul after death that he is concerned with, though Othello himself at the end of the play considers that his soul has been ensnared as though Iago were indeed thus concerned. What Iago aims to do is to destroy love and trust for Othello and the joy that these create for him here and now on earth. He would pour 'pestilence' into his ears and bring hell's pains to him in the body. Yet he would do so in the way of those devils who are most skilfully and effectively devoted to the enlargement of hell hereafter by instigation to blackest sin:

> When devils will the blackest sins put on,
> They do suggest at first with heavenly shows,
> As I do now   (II. iii. 357–9).

The last time Iago invites being thought of as a devil and yet avoids making a sure claim to devilhood is when he is brought in to face Othello as Othello looks upon the dead Desdemona and sees himself as damned—whipped by fiends from the sight of her face. What comes then is final intensification of the effect that Iago has been achieving in many ways with his ambidexterity. Othello turns his sword against him after saying one of the most unforgettable things in the play:

> I look down towards his feet—but that's a fable.
> If that thou be'st a devil, I cannot kill thee
>   (v. ii. 286–7).

And Iago is not killed.

It is true that Othello is interfered with as he strikes. Lodovico has said, 'Wrench his sword from him.' Yet there is room left for a suspicion, and it is plain that Iago is made by Shakespeare to accept the opportunity provided for use of it. When he responds to Othello by saying, 'I bleed, sir, but not kill'd', he might as well be saying, 'Now you see, sir, I cannot be killed.'

7

Iago, a dubious claimant of devilhood, shows in its most diabolic form a capacity of the Shakespearean grotesque to develop enmity toward the non-grotesque. Caliban, with a clear right to devilhood as an inheritor from his sire, exhibits the enmity in a strangely ambiguous way and falls much below Iago in diabolic quality. But Caliban is far from showing a final falling off in Shakespearean grotesque conception. Standing apart not merely from Iago but from all other Shakespearean grotesque figures, he gains as much as he loses by his singularity. His grotesqueness is capable of winning high praise even in the early eighteenth century. Nicholas Rowe, after bowing apologetically in the direction of rational Truth, can call the 'wild Image' that is Caliban 'one of the finest and most uncommon Grotesques that was ever seen'.[1]

Though the grotesque companions of Caliban in *The Tempest* have much to be said for them in their own right, they perhaps serve best as constituting a foil against which Caliban is set off. Stephano and Trinculo are in some ways followers of an early style of Shakespearean grotesque and in other ways contributors to a late style. In all ways they constantly remind us that Caliban shows greater transformation in the Shakespearean grotesque than it has undergone before, early or late.

I have said that Caliban gains by his singularity but loses also. What he most noticeably loses is almost all of that particular comicality in perception and expression which before his appearance might seem to have become essential to the Shakespearean grotesque. He has nothing whatever of the appeal of the clown or jester except when he is seduced by Stephano and turns to drunken song. By nature he speaks as a poet. He has even been given a simple high seriousness and can often win from us a response comparable with that we give to those in the play who by nature are non-grotesque in perception and expression because they have been created to form a company of the high. For Stephano and Trinculo it is as natural to use prose as it is generally for Shakespeare's grotesque figures. For Caliban it is natural to use blank verse, even when he is with Stephano and Trinculo.

Part of the comicality Caliban loses is of a kind that had become

---

[1] In the essay, 'Some Account of the Life &c of Mr. William Shakespeare', introductory to his edition of Shakespeare's *Works*, 1709, i, p. xxiv.

traditionally fitting for the low ranks of the army of evil. There is nothing of the Vice about him. He not only is not a sportive tempter and entrapper of others but does not have any of the quality that makes even Iago play the attendant fool's part by turning off impromptu rhymes for Desdemona as she waits for the landing of Othello at Cyprus. Yet neither does the diabolic Caliban have in place of a Vice's comicality any heritage of supernatural awesomeness from his father. This son of the devil and a witch is of another order entirely from that of the witches of devilish extraction in *Macbeth*. Though he is far from being a mere clownish pretender to evil status, his world is after all that to which in *Macbeth* the hell porter belongs. It is a world of lowness into which in *The Tempest* he is inevitably drawn.

For though he is no jester, he is of course a natural butt for jesters. Stephano and Trinculo make the most of counting themselves his betters. They grant him instruction to help him extend the possibilities of his lowness, looking down upon him all the while for needing the extension.

But in one very notable way Caliban is able to reverse matters and be their leader in supporting the cause of the low. He plans, and gets Stephano and Trinculo to join, a revolutionary action against the high. This they might be expected rather particularly not to engage in, since they seem at first sight to have inherited a basically amiable nature from the early Shakespearean attendant buffoon of non-diabolic cast. Before Caliban, as we have seen, even the Shakespearean grotesque figure of diabolic cast does not come to the point of plotting revolution to overthrow a non-grotesque order, however much he may wish harm or do harm to individual members of that order and to their codes of high endeavour. The diabolically grotesque Caliban is exceptional in being a revolutionary, and he is able to make the non-diabolically grotesque Stephano and Trinculo into revolutionaries even more exceptional. It is Stephano who is truly converted. Trinculo merely follows, not always uncritically, after Stephano.

Behind Caliban as launcher of a revolution there is the early clown Jack Cade in *2 Henry VI*. But in him there is little that points forward to Caliban's kind of grotesqueness. Nor is there much that points forward to Stephano as the would-be king into which Caliban changes him. The dramatic treatment of Cade in his pretentious bid for kingship is one of harshly satiric rejection, not one of comic acceptance in the dominant vein of Shakespearean grotesque creation that produces all three of the revolutionaries in *The Tempest*.

In his inner constitution Caliban has evil derived from both his devil father and his witch mother. Here there is an unknowing lowness that shows no Satanic sophistication gained from his father and no human sophistication gained from his mother. In his bodily form he has a lowness of monstrosity. Here an incomplete creation is implied. He has a combination of bodies instead of finished form in one body, as though forces of nature were of two minds what to make of him when they ceased shaping him. Nor is he of advanced form in any of the bodies of which he is made. He is 'half a fish' (III. ii. 32). Much is suggested of grossness in this half. In the rest of him he is man. But as man he is not only joined with a creature of such low order as a peculiarly unprepossessing kind of fish but has an excess of brute nature in his humanity and is in many respects an undeveloped savage. Trinculo, the professional fool, jealously piqued by Caliban's worship of Stephano as a god, can cry down Caliban as having such unnatural lowness that he is only a natural, a natural-born fool: 'That a monster should be such a natural!' (III. ii. 36-7.) Both Trinculo and Stephano never have the slightest understanding that in Caliban's savage humanity there is reach beyond theirs, however grotesquely unknowing he may be and however grotesquely knowing they may be.

Stephano when we first see him is no more revolutionary than Falstaff, or than others in an early Shakespearean setting who are grotesque accepters or even well-wishers of an established order of the high. At the beginning of *The Tempest* Stephano is as happy as Falstaff to live in a world controlled by the high where there are gratifications to be won by ingenuity and especially where ingenuity can make its owner proud of being able to change bad happening into good. His getting ashore from the supposedly wrecked ship with support from a floating cask of sack and his drawing afterward of further support from the contents of the cask constitute a truly Falstaffian victory over Fortune. There is indication enough that Stephano has originally found no reason for, nor been by nature inclined toward, revolt against those over him. The King of Naples, recognizing him at the end of the play as 'my drunken butler', shows no angry surprise at his servant's drunkenness and seems to have been a tolerant master. At the beginning of the play, when Caliban's worship ('prithee, be my god') begins to expand Stephano's conception of himself, Stephano still retains recognition of the King and others as properly having been above him. For a time he thinks merely of possessing good things of the island that would normally have been theirs: 'Trinculo, the King and all our company else being drown'd, we will inherit here' (II. ii. 178–80).

It takes a specific proposal of action, coming from Caliban later, to make a revolutionary of Stephano. But always, as between him and Caliban, Stephano is the lesser revolutionary. For Stephano there is to be only the killing of a wizard presumed to be vulnerable and the capture of a 'brave lass', the wizard's daughter, in order to set himself up as a king well provided with a queen. But for Caliban there is to be revolution with a sacred purpose. After the overthrow of a tyrannical human ruler there is to be a god established in his place who can uplift a subject's spirit with divine spirit. 'The liquor is not earthly' that this god dispenses. It can communicate the ultimate revolutionary vision of 'Freedom, high-day! high-day, freedom!' (II. ii. 190.)

Yet this Caliban, who as a slave has no longing to turn the tables and dominate, but who simply aspires to be free and in freedom to have communion with a god worthy of worship, is vicious when he comes to think of methods of killing that can be used against those he would have out of his way. It is merely the ferocious beast in Caliban that begs his god Stephano to turn upon the scoffing Trinculo and 'bite him to death', and it is merely the savage primitive man in him that suggests to this god that he

could paunch the sleeping Prospero with a stake, or batter his skull
with a log, or cut his wezand with a knife. It must be added, however, that the implication with regard to Caliban's nature in these
proposals is modified in his suggestion that as Prospero sleeps
Stephano may 'knock a nail into his head'. Here Caliban is given
once again the conception of a murder to be savagely executed but
now with some connotation of its having about it a primitive Old
Testament righteousness. For it was thus with a nail that Jael, wife
of Heber the Kenite, killed the sleeping Sisera, who had become
an enemy of God by being an enemy of God's chosen people
(Judges 4: 21-3). Shakespeare often enough seems willing to balk
some downright condemnation of Caliban that has come to
appear justifiable.

8

What Shakespeare has made of Caliban, Stephano, and Trinculo is the more fully recognized if one looks at it beside what
Dryden and Davenant have made of them in adapting *The Tempest* to Restoration taste. Dryden says that Davenant 'design'd the
Counterpart to Shakespear's Plot, namely that of a Man who had
never seen a Woman' and that the 'Comical parts of the Saylors
were also his invention and for the most part his writing'.[1] These
comical parts form a subplot that is much more truly subordinate
than the corresponding subplot in Shakespeare's play, though it
has larger content. In it Stephano appears with his old name, not
as a butler but as no less than master of the ship upon which Prospero has exercised his magic, and Trinculo appears with the slightly
changed name of Trincalo, not as a jester but as boatswain of the
ship. Caliban now brings in with him a twin sister monstrous as
himself, named Sycorax after their mother. Besides her there are
added to the subplot Mustacho, as Stephano's mate on the ship,
and Ventoso, as a mariner in the crew.

In this revision of a Shakespearean world of lowness Stephano,
Trinculo, and Caliban have parts to play that weaken or frequently
even destroy former bonds between their world and the world of

---

[1] *The Tempest, or the Enchanted Island*, 1670, sig. A2.

the high. The result makes it appear that the Shakespearean grotesque has come to be foreign to Dryden and Davenant. They show here an inclination to hold the grotesque well apart from the non-grotesque and to deal with it condescendingly after a fashion that is not at all Shakespeare's in *The Tempest* nor characteristically his elsewhere.

Just as might be expected, Caliban is the grotesque figure that suffers most at their hands. He has much the most to lose. It is true that with them his past remains as it is recounted in Shakespeare's play except that what has made Prospero abandon kindness toward him and become a severe and much hated taskmaster is an attempt by Caliban to violate not only Miranda but also a second daughter named Dorinda, equally unacquainted with the world of men, who has been acquired by Prospero in the making over of the play. Here, one may say, significant change is hardly to be found in Caliban. There is only more of a nature he has had before. But in what he is as Dryden and Davenant show him on the stage there is very significant change.

There he is no longer a grotesque half-man ironically capable of deeper understanding than any possessed by two grotesque whole men who patronize him. He has fallen to a state where he is little better than his patronizers take him to be. Some of the poetic Caliban still remains, though not much. But nothing remains of the Caliban who creates a revolution because of aspiration to have a benevolent god as master instead of a vicious human tyrant. The new Caliban possesses neither the aspiration nor the ability to create a revolution. Yet he hates Prospero in the way of the old Caliban.

Nor does anyone else that is in the new company of the grotesque start a rebellion against the ascendancy of the non-grotesque. Dryden and Davenant seem to have regarded Shakespeare's presentation of such a rebellion as unedifying. They devise instead an action of power-seizure and rebellion safely confined among the grotesque. It begins when Stephano, thinking that he, Mustacho, and Ventoso are alone on the island, sets up a government. He declares that he has been 'Master at Sea and will be Duke on Land'.

Then Trincalo appears and a challenge to authority is issued. It is Trincalo, not Stephano, who now has come into possession of the butt of sack and has hidden it. With drunken aggressiveness he declares that he will be Duke Trincalo, come what will. Let there be civil war between him and Duke Stephano if there must. Stephano and the others retire, telling Trincalo that if he wishes he can be a rebel all by himself.

At this point Caliban makes his first appearance, carrying wood for Prospero and calling down curses on him. Trincalo wins Caliban's confidence, pours sack down his throat, finds himself worshipped as a god come to earth, and thus gains a subject for his dukedom. He gains a second subject, and likewise a duchess, in Sycorax who has been praised to him by Caliban as his 'lovely Sister, beautiful and bright as the Full Moon' and not to be compared with the daughters of Prospero, for she is 'bigger than 'em both'. This 'Blobber lips', as she turns out to be, Trincalo takes as his spouse in order to strengthen his claim to the island. There is negotiation between the dukedoms of Stephano and Trincalo which seems to be ending with Trincalo's winning dominance by pledging rights for everybody to draw upon his butt of sack. But all promise of peace suddenly fails when Stephano starts to seduce Sycorax. There is a general brawl. Warfare continues as participants leave the scene. Finally Trincalo beats Stephano off the stage and is left alone as a dubious victor, who can think only of guarding his butt of sack and getting rid of Lady Trincalo before she cuckolds him. In the brawl Sycorax has first turned viciously upon him for his action against Stephano, whom she has declared to be her love, and then has beaten Caliban off the stage for bringing about her marriage.

Near the end of the play Dryden and Davenant have a stage direction calling for Ariel to enter 'driving in' the company of the grotesque. The words for what he is to do are the same as those at a corresponding place in Shakespeare's play. But lacking now is an original specification that members of this company are to be dressed 'in their stolen apparel'. The severity implied in the word 'driving' is no longer meant for grotesque attempters of murder who have been turned aside from this atrocious aim only by being shunted into thievery and who must be made to realize their failings. It is now meant merely for grotesque wanderers who must be rounded up for return into the service of their masters. Since the plot to kill Prospero has been omitted, his counterplot to put off his assailants by tempting them with a display of sumptuous garments has also been omitted and no apparel has been stolen. With struggle for power adequately confined, no more serious revolutionary action has been attempted than the overthrow on dry land of a shipmaster by his boatswain while these two were playing at being dukes. They have not even been moved to steal the trappings of a true duke. Stephano transformed from butler into shipmaster and Trinculo transformed from jester into boatswain are signs that the attendant clown and the attendant fool of the Elizabethan stage are dead and that the grotesque is no longer joined closely enough to the non-grotesque to be effectively presumptuous.

As for Caliban, his transformation is from a monstrous underling capable of strange nobilities of spirit into a monstrous underling pure and simple. It indicates a sad falling off in audience appreciation for a Shakespearean grotesque figure that is *sui generis*. Hazlitt has clearly the right of the matter when he says that in Shakespeare's hands Caliban 'acquires a classical dignity' in comparison with Stephano and Trinculo, and that he shows 'the essence of grossness' but 'not a particle of vulgarity'.[1] One may go on to say that in the hands of Dryden and Davenant Caliban loses dignity and gains vulgarity.

9

Perhaps more than any other play of Shakespeare's *The Tempest* leaves us unhappy with an attempt to say what most essentially it is 'about'. It is so rich in suggestion that to speak of its having ruling themes, rather than a central theme, may be excusable. Assuredly one ruling theme in it is love. This covers a range stretching from love between parent and child to love between

[1] William Hazlitt, *Characters of Shakespear's Plays*, London, 1817, pp. 117, 118.

man and woman and finally to love between fellow men that inspires forgiveness of the wrongdoer by the one wronged.

As the theme of love is developed in the play bonds become clear between Caliban, who as a monster is counted lowest among the grotesque, and Ferdinand, who as a king's son is counted one of the highest among the non-grotesque. It is revealed that these two are both young lovers in a romance and are brothers of some sort under the skin. Desire by which they are joined is directed toward the same object. One wins the coveted Miranda and the other does not, but both suffer for love of her. Moreover, they suffer in ways made by Shakespeare so strikingly similar that their being bound together is not to be overlooked.

Near the beginning of the action Caliban is found to be enslaved and confined by Prospero. He is said to have deserved 'more than a prison' for a violent wooing of Miranda that Prospero counts as an attempted rape. Caliban himself counts it as a most natural approach to mating. One owes it to him to recognize that his animal mating urge is not momentary nor blind. He can take progenitive delight in the thought of peopling the island with Calibans and can wish that Prospero had not been able to prevent his doing so. Also, he can see beauty in Miranda that makes her worthy to be the bedfellow of a god and bring forth 'brave brood', as he shows when he recommends sacrificially that she be taken as queen by Stephano. Caliban is not lacking in a lover's poetry of praise. But as he undergoes the suffering of confinement and slavery that comes to him through love he has no high-flown thought that keeping the image of his beloved before his eyes can make that suffering naught. He has only resentment and pours maledictions on Prospero. His confinement is within a rock and his slavery that of carrying wood for fuel in the service of a master who is always ready to punish dereliction with a magical effectiveness.

As the second scene of the second act opens, Caliban enters 'with a burden of wood', thinking of what he suffers at the hand of Prospero. As the next scene opens, Ferdinand enters 'bearing a log', thinking of what he suffers at the hand of Prospero. Ferdinand has been brought to 'wooden slavery' by showing ardent response to the attraction of Miranda, just as Caliban has. Further-more, because of that response, he has been put in prison, just as Caliban has.

But in all of this there are differences as well as likenesses to serve as constant reminders that experience shared by the grotesque and the non-grotesque is given distinctive quality by each. Slavery and imprisonment here are themes subsidiary to the theme of love. They enlarge the area in which likenesses and differences are brought together to be balanced against each other. The wooden slavery is much the same for Caliban as for Ferdinand, except for what each finds in it essentially. The primitively simple Caliban finds in it only something to be fiercely fought against all the while it is endured under compulsion. He accepts it no more than an undomesticated animal would. The civilizedly sophisti-cated Ferdinand, however, finds in it something that the thought-ful man can condemn and yet at the same time readily accept. Recognizing one code of high endeavour developed in his culture Ferdinand can say that 'some kinds of baseness / Are nobly under-gone'. Recognizing another such code, he can go farther and say:

> The mistress which I serve quickens what's dead
> And makes my labours pleasures   (III. i. 6–7).

It is by having a mistress that Ferdinand becomes a slave and a servant, to Miranda as well as to Prospero. Miranda enslaves him for courtly love-service. He tells her:

> The very instant that I saw you, did
> My heart fly to your service; there resides,
> To make me slave to it   (III. i. 64–6).

Prospero enslaves him for log-carrying service on perceiving this love of his for Miranda, 'lest too light winning / Make the prize light'. It is likewise by having a mistress that Ferdinand becomes imprisoned. Resisting his enslavement by Prospero he is confined to inaction by enchantment. But he is confident that he will be granted freedom of spirit by the sight of Miranda's beauty. The beholding of her 'through my prison once a day', he is sure, will give 'space enough' within. Ferdinand's slavery of love and the liberty of love that comes in the midst of enslavement and imprisonment by Prospero are not within the experience or understanding of Caliban in any form.

The theme of power is as strong in *The Tempest* as the theme of love. In ways that force themselves upon one's attention it often is joined with the theme of love. There is a union of the two implied when Prospero decides that the lovers at their first meeting have been put 'both in either's pow'rs'. Another union of the themes is implied in what Ferdinand says when Prospero, to slow the course of this love, falsely accuses him of seeking to capture the island and threatens to put him in manacles. Ferdinand, without knowing the bearing of his words for a master of magical art, challenges Prospero to call up a more than ordinary power for trial against his own more than ordinary power gained through love:

> I will resist such entertainment till
> Mine enemy has more power
>
> (I. ii. 465–6).

The extraordinary power of Prospero makes him, one may say, the human prime mover of action in the play. If the thought comes to the viewer of the play that Prospero is made to suggest a divine prime mover, it may be found to have some basis. As early as the opening of the second scene there is a remark of Miranda's that can raise the thought. When she expresses pity for the suffering of those on the supposedly wrecked ship, she says that had she herself 'been any god of power' she would have sunk the sea within the earth before it should have swallowed this good ship and the souls it carried. She speaks as though her father had apparently just proved himself to be one kind of god of power where she would have been quite another. For she begins her speech by asking him to allay the storm if he has raised it.

Whatever god of power is found to be suggested in Prospero must be granted two aspects, one of harsh severity and the other of clemency and love. In other words, he must be a divinity with aspects well recognized in the Christian tradition. He must have both Old Testament and New Testament characteristics. Prospero is capable of saying to Ferdinand when he finally surrenders Miranda to him that if he has 'too austerely punis'd' him, the 'vexations' meted out 'were but trials' of a lover's love. He is also capable of telling Miranda, when she has been moved to pity by the illusion of the sinking ship, that he has done 'nothing but in care of' her. It turns out that he has done nothing but in care of many who in the end are brought to a finding of themselves at a time 'when no man was his own'. In the end he acknowledges the wrath he has felt because of the 'high wrongs' some of these have done him and yet, 'they being penitent', he turns to mercy with the memorable decision that 'the rarer action is / In virtue than in vengeance' (v. i. 27–8).

But from suggestions like these it will not do to conclude that Prospero 'stands for' God in *The Tempest*. As A. D. Nuttall cogently says, the play 'shimmers between subjectivity and objectivity' and 'will not keep still long enough for one to affix the allegorical label'. But in it, as he also says, 'love *is* conceived as a supernatural force'.[1] And one may add that in it Prospero is at the centre of the workings of this force.

Love is conceived in *The Tempest* as a power working both upon nature and by means of nature. It is in Prospero, and it does its work as he utilizes beings like the elemental Ariel or such 'weak masters' of the areas of nature as 'elves of hills, brooks, standing lakes, and groves' (v. i. 33). But though the power is in Prospero, he recognizes that it is not of him and that he has but part of it. He sees the love between Ferdinand and Miranda as something fostered by him that must also be otherwise sustained: 'Heavens rain grace / On that which breeds between 'em' (III. i. 75–6).

Even in the brutish nature of Caliban Prospero has been able to arouse a love of one kind by stroking him as he would an animal and teaching him words. 'And then I lov'd thee' testifies Caliban. Yet Prospero has not been able to accept for encouragement the

---

[1] *Two Concepts of Allegory: A Study of Shakespeare's 'The Tempest' and the Logic of Allegorical Expression*, London, 1967, p. 159.

beginnings of a love of another kind in Caliban's unsophisticated mating urge. The result for Caliban is hatred of Prospero instead of love, and it eventually brings revolt against all that Prospero is as a figure of power.

Where the theme of power in the play extends to the overthrow or attempted overthrow of power there is further revelation of bonds between the grotesque and the non-grotesque. Here again Caliban is a grotesque figure of outstanding importance.

In telling Miranda the story of her being brought to the island as an infant her father dwells upon the power he once had. As Duke of Milan he was 'a prince of power'. He was overthrown by his brother Antonio, to whom he, while rapt in his studies, had entrusted the office of government, in which lay what he thinks of again as 'my power'. There followed his enforced voyage with Miranda to the island and his exercise in banishment of magical art gained from his continued studies. With this power greater than the princely or ducal he has subjected Ariel and Caliban to his service and moved toward a righting of wrongs. At the beginning of the play we find him making promises of eventual freedom to Ariel but not to Caliban. At first Caliban thinks he can do nothing but obey him hopelessly:

> His art is of such pow'r
> It would control my dam's god, Setebos,
> And make a vassal of him   (I. ii. 372–4).

But then Caliban encounters Stephano and believes that in him he has found a god greater than Setebos and more than a match for Prospero. He plots Prospero's overthrow by the newfound god. Thus a man who is implied to be a god of power by Miranda is paired with and pitted against a man who is confidently taken to be a god of power by Caliban. A deified hero with non-grotesque credentials is to be assailed by one with grotesque credentials. The overthrow by grotesque power with which he is threatened has the possibility of proving greater than that by non-grotesque power which he has already experienced, for his life is now at stake.

In this plot formed by Caliban against Prospero the grotesque conjoins with the non-grotesque in another and very different way. Just before Caliban encounters Stephano and begins to worship the man he will try to make king by suggesting to him the killing of Prospero, a non-grotesque plot is formed which seems to act as a challenge to the company of the grotesque to produce something of the same vicious kind. Antonio, supplanter of his brother Prospero, prefigures the plotter Caliban when he urges Sebastian to supplant his own brother Alonso as King of Naples. No more than Stephano has Sebastian thought of becoming king when the suggestion of overthrowing a ruler is made to him. Antonio plans details for a murder that is to be accomplished while the intended victim is asleep, just as Caliban does, except that Antonio himself engages to kill Alonso but Caliban leaves the killing of Prospero to Stephano. The two plots are completely alike in being vulnerable to a Prospero who has power more than natural to foresee events and to command natural forces in the elemental form of an Ariel.

10

Caliban is created near the end of Shakespeare's career after there has been much transformation of grotesque conception, for Shakespeare and for others before him. But merely so far as his monstrous body is concerned, he would very surely have had a familiar quality for St. Bernard of Clairvaux, whose comment upon the medieval grotesque as he knew it has been the starting-point of discussion in my first chapter. One need not try to determine exactly how the parts of Caliban's body are formed if one is concerned with the essential quality of his outer grotesqueness. There is an embarrassment of different indications for his appearance.[1] The most specific thing said about it is Trinculo's exclamation, 'Legg'd like a man! and his fins like arms!' (II. ii. 33.) And it is perhaps put in most confusing terms when Stephano later calls Caliban a 'man-monster' and Trinculo at the same time calls him

---

[1] An examination of the indications is offered by Audrey Yoder, *Animal Analogy in Shakespeare's Character Portrayal*, New York, 1947, pp. 91 ff.

first a 'debosh'd fish' and then 'but half a fish and half a monster' (III. ii. 30–33). Whatever the difficulty in interpreting such remarks, a general implication in all of them taken together is clear enough. It is that Caliban is a Renaissance dramatic version of what has been called the 'hybrid' figure in medieval grotesque art, a much favoured form of which I have already taken account as having been given endless variety, especially in illuminations upon manuscript margins.[1] To say so is not to suggest that Shakespeare as he created Caliban needed to look anywhere but within himself to draw upon a grotesque tradition that could be helpful. In many ways this had come to be part of him.

It is to the shaping of the inner Caliban, not the outer, that Shakespeare gives the best of himself. But the inner has some accord with the outer in its doubleness. With a body that is part primitive man and part crude fish Caliban may be said to show externally, for all to see, a version of that strange union of the more-than-animal and the merely-animal which is a finding within man in general. The inner union thus represented for him is akin, though on a much lower plane for both parts, to that in Hamlet's vision of man as a possessor both of godlike reason and of bestial compulsion to sleep and feed. It makes a monster similarly grotesque in the incompatibility of its parts.

Within Caliban there is another union of a somewhat similar kind that is also recognized in man generally. This is the union of good and evil. In Caliban it takes on a special character and has an extraordinary grotesqueness in the incompatibility of its parts. His evil is offered as being extreme in that it is an inheritance from a father the very essence of evil and a mother lost to evil. Prospero, as he takes steps to save himself from the assassination plotted by Caliban, gives up all hope of regeneration for him:

> A devil, a born devil, on whose nature

[1] The figure is called 'hybrid' by Lilian M. C. Randall, *Images in the Margins of Gothic Manuscripts*, Berkeley and Los Angeles, 1966. In this book there is a helpful index of grotesque forms, with references to manuscripts in which examples are to be found. More than half of the many listings under the letter 'H' are of various hybrid forms. For reproductions of some of these see Figures 236 ff.

Nurture can never stick! on whom my pains,
Humanely taken, all, all lost, quite lost!

(IV. i. 188–90.)

But here it is the harshly severe in Prospero that speaks. For in making judgement thus he takes no account of that in Caliban which we can find to be averse from evil, even to the point of truest innocence, and yet be intricately joined with it. Caliban is a born devil only in the way of the ordinary hyperbole, though fathered as he has been. His evil is the evil of a man, which after all he is fully made to be in the action of the play, and his diabolism, as I have said, is very far from having the inhuman quality of Iago's. He is no Iagoesque enemy of love, but instead a simple beginner in the practice of love, even of love that leads to worship.

11

At the conclusion of *The Tempest* Caliban is made to come close to, if not to arrive at, desertion of the company of the grotesque. As Prospero finally tempers justice with mercy for those who have wronged him, he issues a command to Caliban. Caliban is to take his fellow conspirators, Stephano and Trinculo, with him to Prospero's cell, where the three of them are to do service needed, giving it the best of attention. Prospero holds out hope of forgiveness:

> As you look
> To have my pardon, trim it handsomely.

Caliban replies:

> Ay, that I will! and I'll be wise hereafter,
> And seek for grace. What a thrice-double ass
> Was I to take this drunkard for a god
> And worship this dull fool!

(V. i. 292–7.)

Stephano and Trinculo, who have previously confessed discomfiture, now say nothing. We are confident that they remain as enduringly marked with the sign of the grotesque as Falstaff remains at the time of his banishment. As to what is to be thought of Caliban when he speaks these last words heard from him, we find ourselves in disagreement. For instance, Bonamy Dobrée can say firmly of the Caliban who promises to be wise and seek for grace that 'we are not impressed', but G. Wilson Knight can say just as firmly that 'he has moved from black magic, through nature and man, to grace'.[1]

Certainly Caliban, who is capable of simple earnestness and is never a rogue delighting in deception, is a better candidate than Autolycus for the role of a grotesque recalcitrant brought to the verge of reform by the spirit of reconciliation in Shakespearean tragicomedy. Autolycus confers benefits upon others in *The Winter's Tale* against his will, as he himself says. He insists that he is not 'naturally honest', though he is so 'sometimes by chance'. He is a descendant of the Vice Ambidexter in the morality play *Cambises* in so far as he comes to find himself at the end of the play rather amazedly playing with both hands and doing good as well as evil. Opportunity is offered him to procure benefits by changing his way of life, and he promises to reform 'to my power'. But we are convinced that he must remain grotesque, even if he is taken into the world of the non-grotesque. The offerer of opportunity to him, the son of the shepherd foster-father of Perdita, glories in having become a 'gentleman born' after having been a born clown, but he has suffered no loss of grotesqueness. He makes us feel sure that Autolycus, if raised in status, would be just as able to avoid transformation. He asks of Autolycus, 'Thou wilt amend thy life?' But he says he knows Autolycus will not, even as he goes on to promise sponsorship for him:

> If it be ne'er so false, a true gentleman may swear it in the behalf of his friend. And I'll swear to the Prince thou art a tall fellow of thy hands, and that thou wilt not be drunk; but I know thou art no tall fellow of thy hands, and that thou wilt be drunk. But I'll swear it
>
> (v. ii. 175–80).

[1] Bonamy Dobrée, 'The Tempest', *Essays and Studies*, ed. Arundell Esdaile, London, 1952, p. 16; G. Wilson Knight, *The Crown of Life: Essays in Interpretation of Shakespeare's Final Plays*, London, 1947, p. 239.

Yet however much more possible some of us may think true reformation to be for Caliban than for Autolycus, the effective contribution of the one no less than the other to the drama containing him comes obviously from possession and practice of grotesqueness, not from development toward rejection of grotesqueness. It goes without saying that for Shakespeare's grotesque figures aside from these two the effective dramatic contribution takes form in the same way. In them, moreover, there is nothing at all to be considered seriously as importing eventual change of heart. Each has the secure faith expressed by Parolles in *All's Well that Ends Well* that 'place and means' are provided for him in the scheme of life and that he is called upon to be what he is. Even Iago looks upon himself as well favoured with opportunity to be himself. He can be confident that what is responsible for the existence of evil in life gives support to a share of evil in grotesqueness, including the direst evil. In Shakespeare's world the provision of place and means for Iago and Thersites, with their unrelieved nay-saying, is markedly similar to that for Falstaff and Lear's fool, with their intricate combinations of nay-saying and yea-saying.

INDEX

PRINTED IN GREAT BRITAIN
AT THE UNIVERSITY PRESS, OXFORD
BY VIVIAN RIDLER
PRINTER TO THE UNIVERSITY